When the Cathedrals Were White

For nearly sixty years Le Corbusier,
along with Frank Lloyd Wright and Walter
Gropius, has been in the forefront of
modern architecture. In this book the
distinguished architect focuses on American
architecture, its ugliness and charm.

TRANSLATED FROM THE FRENCH:

QUAND LES CATHÉDRALES ETÁIENT BLANCHES

BY FRANCIS E. HYSLOP, JR.

When the Cathedrals Were White
Le Corbusier

McGraw-Hill Book Company
New York   Toronto   London

TO MY MOTHER,

woman of courage and faith

CONTENTS

WHEN THE CATHEDRALS
WERE WHITE

INTRODUCTION
TO THE AMERICAN TRANSLATION

The American Army, arrived in Europe, found its lands, its peoples, its cities, and its fields ravaged by four years of war, emptied and robbed, in ruins, covered with dirt and eaten with rust; found broken windows and nerves on edge, exhausted bodies and tenacious morale. American aviators had bombed everything, blowing up bridges, stations, railroads, factories, ports. There was no wax for the floors, no paint for rooms and houses, no soap to wash with. In the Paris subway, the only means of transportation for five million persons, faces were green from privations. And in Paris (it was only known afterward) the Germans had executed seventy-five thousand men and women, after having tortured them.

On the day of liberation a portion of the armies of the USA and of Leclerc's army passed through Boulogne-sur-Seine, the suburb of Paris in which I was living. A terrible hour to live through, feelings in tumult and tears in our eyes. A spectacle: those men, boys from the United States on magisterial machines, twenty-year-old boys who had just beaten the enemy. Near them, Leclerc's soldiers who had come from Lake Chad, having crossed the Sahara; tomorrow, in a single bound, they would move on to Berchtesgaden; engraved on their faces they bore the tradition of two thousand martial years. The women of the suburb, like those in all of Paris, had dressed in their prettiest in anticipation of the liberation. They were adorned with smiles and joy. The women of Paris had been extraordinary: without dressmaking materials, without means of maintaining their customary elegance, they managed the trick of being desirable; without hats, they had invented ways of turning their hair into gold, bronze, or ebony helmets, a warlike coiffure which made them luminous and magnificent. Feminine centaurs on bicycles cutting through the fog of Paris in the springtime or in the dog days, legs, hair, faces, breasts whipped by the wind, indifferent but disturbing, they passed under the noses of the sinister-purposed, drearily colored "green mustard" soldiers. . . .

They climbed up the American tanks; they kissed the Americans, leaving lipstick on dusty cheeks; they sat down beside the crews and drivers. Alas, they were taken for whores!

The children, naturally, were on the guns, on the turrets, on the knees of soldiers. Many asked for cigarettes. Some of them were greedy. The soldiers called the French beggars! For four years they had had only two or three packs a month, which is more tormenting than not smoking at all. If the authorities had had the courage, they would have simply cut off tobacco. After two months of annoyance everyone would have been free of that nagging desire.

O Americans, soldiers of the United States suddenly landed on morally and physically exhausted countries, on countries where all goods had become ersatz, controlled by nearly worthless ration points, in physical misery and shabbily dressed, to you, accustomed to unheard-of abundance and frightening waste,

Europe—the great country of your fathers—seemed dirty, cut to pieces. Mad with joy, Europe welcomed you; you thought her indecent!

In the United States your cities are strong and rich. New York is the home of some god of modern life; a perhaps still nameless god. Your towns are painted with white and with intense colors; they have no confining walls: the lawns extend from house to house like a luxurious carpet under well-kept trees.

You were astonished, you were shocked: "Is this Paris, is this Europe?"

Coming from the south on the same day of liberation, Leclerc's tanks, moving in a direction opposite to that of De Gaulle's procession, went up the Champs Elysées, on the heels of the enemy. On the sides of the tanks supplied to our army, in large, freshly painted white letters, were names of French provinces (France was being liberated by the minute!!!): Brittany, Provence, Flanders; names of the great of France: Vercingetorix, Bayard, Joan of Arc, Lafayette; names of French qualities: courage, valor, fidelity. . . .

On the occasion of this hasty passage before the Arch of Triumph, and for the sake of dignifying the taking over of this magnificent machinery of war by sans-culottes, you were right, leaders, in thus affirming essential values. And you were right in organizing the march past the arch of triumphs, where the tomb of the unknown soldier is placed. The tomb is immaterial architecture except for a flame and a dedication on the level of the ground. A monument reaching the scale without any possible measure of the ordeal endured. When, in this book, the white cathedrals are called up as witnesses on the side of modern times, this monument takes an unrivaled place; it reveals the spirit. Who imagined it? Who suggested it? I do not know; it is not known; I believe that no one (or very nearly) yet knows.

American friends, among those of you who have spent some time in France there are some who have entered more deeply into French existence. You have knocked at certain doors and found plain men who, through forty years of effort, or thirty, or twenty, have brought spirit into the world, have made the buds of the present mutation bloom: the artists, the great artists who, in the millennial humus of Paris, have caused the germination of the great metamorphosis which can make radiant tomorrows.

Some of you went to these men as fervent friends. But others were autograph hunters.

The authorities (yours and ours), feeling how necessary it was that we know each other, exchanged smiles and gestures of courtesy. American students were enrolled in France and French students in America. Intellectual exchanges. Who controlled them? God or the Devil? Life or the Academy? I know American students of painting and architecture placed in the big schools who said to me: "We went through that once and that is enough!" The time they spent in other parts of the city, fortunately, will bear fruit.

Academy—Life, that is the question! That remains the question in the USA as in France, as in the whole world.

Life creates and destroys; it gives birth to the temples of India and also to the creeping tropical plants which will loosen stone from stone in the work men have failed to guard.

Life has made New York, "a vertical city." And with joy we have saluted this city of life.

The skyscrapers are high. Here height is an automatic result of mechanical calculation, of the financial balance sheet, and of publicity. Between the ground and the top of the skyscraper spirit was not called in, but only number. You must look at the top, seek the intention, see what the spiritual reality of the enterprise is. The top is the cork of the bottle that architecture and architects have fashioned with care. As examples I see three of them before me, against the sky. One reproduces the Château of Blois in Touraine; another was inspired by the Sainte Chapelle; the third has the slate, roof, and chimneys of Fountainebleau. Ugh, ugh! Take care that that spirit, misusing height, money, and publicity, does not lay claim to the leadership of the spiritual destinies of the USA!

On Sunday the city ceases to be anything, the streets being empty and the buildings deprived of their meaning (except for Rockefeller Center and several others in which there is architectural life). Sunday is an astonishing touchstone which, for twenty-four hours, can cause the collapse of this magnificent city which, in its essence, is still a Babel.

In contrast, in other places where life seeks nourishment, honky-tonks and juke box joints, in Harlem and on Broadway, laughing jazz rises to the attack. . . .

Men of the United States, you are Americans, and Americans are all the peoples of the world; and this world can be the new world crowning the New World.

Before the war, all the editors who considered the publication of Marguerite Tjader Harris's skillful and intelligent translation of *Quand Les Cathédrales Etaient Blanches* (published in part in issues of *Direction*, 1938, 1939), had insisted on dropping the first fifty pages, which have to do with France. Since then your armies have been among us and, naturally, the first fifty pages will remain in this new translation. Between the lines you will discover the premonitory symptoms of a defeat. There was a menace; there were deadly germs; there was the dangerous academic spirit.

In Paris, in this spring of '46, sap is circulating in hearts and heads. Do you think that such an ordeal has made such a country bow? A squaring of accounts is in process; there a debate about the reasons for living has opened. The long ordeal was an irresistible ferment: heads and hearts acquired energy in going through it and, since the core of the sickness has been struck down, there is a passionate will to climb up as high as possible.

In six years France has gone through a pathetic cycle. She is preparing herself to choose, to determine, to decide; but wavering steps may continue. We do not lightly enter such new paths!

When I was invited to come to the United States for the first time, by the Museum of Modern Art, I was considered the man of "the machine for living" and also as the man who had said: "The skyscrapers of New York are too small." It was held against me, I was treated a little coolly.

Ten years have passed. The misunderstanding is disappearing; understanding seems to be growing; our positions are becoming stabilized, as when the water has risen in one side of a lock: the levels are equal, the gates open, the ships pass through, ideas circulate.

The American potential which has sprung up in the course of the century, which has drawn an unimaginable profit from the two wars, is an event overflowing and exceeding the present limits of material and moral control, just as, at the other end of the world also, in the USSR, an equally powerful but different potential has begun a series of events whose repercussions are unpredictable. Thus far neither the one nor the other of these forces is clear-sighted; they are quite simply on the march, getting under way. And, on the march, they commit and will commit excesses, just as they bring and will bring all the reasons for hope and all the proofs of efficacity. Nevertheless they roll on, and through lack of adjustment, they cause paradoxical results, specific maladies, dangerous fevers.

Thus, for instance, the detestable gift of unlimited means of transporting people and ideas: mobility turned into a disease, a disease that might be called m-o-b-i-l-i-t-i-s,—*mobilitis*.

Everything rolls here; motors roar on water, on highways, on railroads, and in the air; men are on wheels; they have wheels under their bottoms and thus they transgress the law of nature—of human nature, which is eminently alternating and not continuous: footsteps, the beating of heart and arteries, the closing of eyelids, the breathing of the lungs and the formulation of speech, etc. . . . For the philosophic spectator, the end of the road quickly appears: as things are, the cycle of the actions of life is not carried out, or not fully, or with pain and loss, in the irre-

missible period of time of each day. That is the judge, that is the
touchstone: daily life. And here is the verdict: incompleteness,
dissatisfaction, injury written into the overcrowded solar day,
recurring each day and impoverishing each day, and consequently
into the whole life of men. The family torn apart, a kind of
alcoholism, are among the elements in the vague outline which
surrounds the unfolding of this drama.

How to live? The problem does not exist in countries that
are unaware of it, but only for those who see clearly. And it is
the binomial equation *individual-collectivity* which requires an
effective, radiant harmony. The limits of freedom have to be
determined, though fixing limits may seem necessarily to strike
out freedom, which is not the case. The liberties of some, like
the intangibility of certain principles, are becoming objects of
discussion and examination. Indeed, the disorder is evident
throughout American life in what in '35 I called "The Great
Waste." The word waste could be associated with the French
term *emptying*. Applied to social life, emptying is a disaster, a
death march. At the present time, and especially in America, it
appears in the form of four daily hours of slavery demanded of
everyone in order to pay the costs of urban chaos.

Knowing how to live is the fundamental question before
modern society, everywhere, in the whole world. An ingenuous
question and one that could be considered childish. How to
live? Do you know how, reader? Do you know how to live
soundly, strongly, gaily, free of the hundred stupidities established by habit, custom, and urban disorganization?

If this book had to wait ten years for an American publisher,
I should like to be able to congratulate myself about it, since on
my return from the USA in 1936 I realized that it was necessary
to invent a sign which might serve as a guide, as a Table of the
Law. Then, in 1937, in the center of the Pavilion of the New
Times at the International Exposition of Arts and Techniques,
on a table dominated by the large open book which set forth the
Charter of Athens of the International Congresses of Modern
Architecture, I had this sign painted:

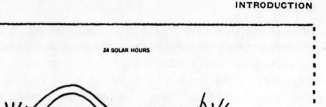

and had this statement inscribed: *This is the measure of our urban enterprises.*

If, in the course of the mutation of machine civilization, I have been able to contribute something, as a person with some rationality and intelligence, as a technician, as a thoughtful man, it will be this sign.

If I can be useful in some way to the United States now, it is in commending this sign to the meditation of those whose mission it is to see clearly and lead. I offer this sign as a measuring instrument which can give the right dimensions to the new centers of production developing from the reconversion of war industries: the substance of society, with all its rights and duties, is being taken up into our hands again. I know that here I am on the essential theme, the great modern theme: HABITATION, knowing how to live in a place. Habitation is life, knowing how to live! How to use the blessings of God: the sun and the spirit that He has given to men to enable them to achieve the joy of living on earth and to find again the Lost Paradise.

To whom am I speaking? *To whom it may concern.* Who is concerned . . . ? That is the usefulness of books: they go out and find *those who are concerned.* Someday, behind the Americans, the youth of the whole world will decide!

City planning (city planning and architecture are inseparable from one another, they make up a single phenomenon) is the social organizer par excellence.

About 1935 the work of the TVA was begun. In January of this year, '46, I went to see its effects. Man and nature, laws of nature and calculations which also express the laws of the world, human imagination in search of harmony . . . Neglect had unloosed catastrophic events in the valley. Things were going from bad to worse. Nature was taken by the hand and finally her anger was calmed; once again she became maternal. The cyclic flow of water brought about a wonderful regeneration; men found again abundance and the promise of joy. And also, in mastering nature, they felt pride in having created the great dams which are bearers of physical and spiritual splendor.

Ten years were enough to bring about the appeasement of hostile forces and the alliance of man and his setting.

I am writing these lines in New York where I arrived twenty hours after leaving Paris. Sometimes, from a great height, I saw a gigantic iceberg in the dark blue ocean, a witness of physical realities and a segment of a regular cycle.

Man, nature, cosmos, those are the given elements.

One day (a hundred years ago), man went from the immemorial speed of walking to the unlimited speeds of machines. Everything was called in question. The limits of control were torn away, extended to the point of disappearing. But the sun, imperturbable in its course, continued to mark the rhythm of our work. Today it accuses us of confusion, lack of foresight, neglect, heedlessness; misfortune and the worst kind of disproportion are the result.

In January of this year I came here in nineteen days, through storms, in an empty freighter, in order to carry out a small mission with Claudius.

When we arrived in Manhattan, pilgrims who had gone through years of grief, affliction, frustration, we experienced a frightful shock: the collision of people who cannot really bring together the things they have lived through—ours, sad ones, theirs, extravagant abundance. Thus, the merchandise that we bring today cannot be taken from the stock of the miseries we have gone through; it can be only constructive discovery, clear, rational, representing our proposals for the future—the wise future of machine society in search of its welfare . . . lost but recoverable and discoverable before us, in the future, in an immediate tomorrow. Geography speaks, then: USA and USSR; at the geographic and historical heart: Paris, capital of a France fortunately well rooted in her own soil, the eye (on the map) of a united Europe. Today this third trip to New York gives me the impression and the certainty that the earth is round and continuous and things contiguous. A master unity will be established.

We French, then, who have had the cathedrals and Louis XIV, can admire the prodigious work, which is still in process of birth, accomplished by the people of America. Humbly I take off my hat. Night or day, at each step in New York—a fairy catastrophe—I find pretexts for reflection, for mental construction, for dreams of extraordinary, cheering, happy tomorrows near at hand. There is hope in the world. With full hands this country of the timid people gives us causes for hope.

I am one of a commission whose task is to find a permanent site for the United Nations in the neighborhood of New York. Harmony is the purpose of the United Nations. Harmony will be achieved by making organizational effectiveness (or efficiency) secure along with respect for the individual human being—more than that, by bringing the joy of living into being through wise city planning, a science which today is becoming a key, the key.

As yet no one knows surely whether or not such an affirmation is tenable, and still less whether or not it is the means by which the men of the second period of machine civilization, after having acted like gangsters and madmen, will set their house in order again.

LE CORBUSIER

New York, May 21, 1946.

PREFACE

This book also [1] will be full of tumult because the world today is full of tumult, because everything is unchained.

It is noon on a summer day; I am driving at full speed along the quays of the Left Bank toward the Eiffel Tower, under the ineffable blue sky of Paris. My eye fixes for a second a white point in the sky; the new tower of Chaillot. I slow down, I look, I plunge suddenly into the depths of time: Yes, the cathedrals were white, completely white, dazzling and young—and not black, dirty, old. The whole period was fresh and young.

[1] "La Ville Radieuse," published in 1935, has to do with the equipping of machine age civilization in the city and in the country. That book is the fruit of fifteen years of work; it is dense; it is like a cellar filled with every kind of food. I have been reproached for it. Even today I am unable to preside over a polite drawing room where etiquette is queen.

. . . And today, yes! today also is young, fresh, new. Today also the world is beginning again. . . .

I have just returned from the USA. Good! I am going to show through the USA, taken as an example, that the times are new, but that its living quarters are uninhabitable. The table has not been cleared after dinner; the remains of a banquet have been allowed to lie in disorder after the departure of the guests: cold sauces, picked bones, wine spots, crumbs, and dirty silver scattered about.

The cathedrals belong to France, and Manhattan is American. What a good opportunity to consider this fresh, twenty-year-old city against the background of one's awareness of the skyscrapers of God. This new place in the world, New York, examined by a heart full of the sap of the Middle Ages. Middle Ages? That is where we are today: the world to be put in order, to be put in order on piles of debris, as was done once before on the debris of antiquity, when the cathedrals were white.

Nevertheless, before opening the window on that landscape of time, I shall first have you breathe the exhausting atmosphere in which we are struggling. The pages about the USA will be, rather than a narrative, the considered reaction of a man lifted up by hope for times of strength and harmony. Today, finally, in the history of the world, the page turns.

Paris, June 1936.

PART ONE
ATMOSPHERES

1 GREATNESS OF THINGS

WHEN THE CATHEDRALS WERE WHITE

I should like to bring to an examination of conscience and to repentance those who, with all the ferocity of their hatred, of their fright, of their poverty of spirit, of their lack of vitality, concern themselves with a fatal stubbornness in the destruction and hindrance of whatever is most beautiful in this country—France —and in this period: the invention, the courage, and the creative genius occupied especially with questions of building—with those things in which reason and poetry co-exist, in which wisdom and enterprise join hands.

When the cathedrals were white, Europe had organized the crafts under the imperative impulse of a quite new, marvelous, and exceedingly daring technique the use of which led to unexpected systems of forms—in fact to forms whose spirit disdained the legacy of a thousand years of tradition, not hesitating to thrust civilization toward an unknown adventure. An international language reigned wherever the white race was, favoring the exchange of ideas and the transfer of culture. An international style had spread from the West to the East and from the North to the South—a style which carried with it the passionate stream of spiritual delights: love of art, disinterestedness, joy of living in creating.

The cathedrals were white because they were new. The cities were new; they were constructed all at once, in an orderly way, regular, geometric, in accordance with plans. The freshly cut stone of France was dazzling in its whiteness, as the Acropolis in Athens had been white and dazzling, as the Pyramids of Egypt had gleamed with polished granite. Above all the cities and towns encircled by new walls, the skyscrapers of God dominated the countryside. They had made them as high as possible, extraordinarily high. It may seem a disproportion in the ensemble. Not at all, it was an act of optimism, a gesture of courage, a sign of pride, a proof of mastery! In addressing themselves to God, men did not sign their own abdication.

The new world was beginning. White, limpid, joyous, clean, clear, and without hesitations, the new world was opening up like a flower among the ruins. They left behind them all recognized ways of doing things; they turned their backs on all that. In a hundred years the marvel was accomplished and Europe was changed.

The cathedrals were white.

Let us bring to life in our imaginations this joyful spectacle. Let us stop a moment to read these lines and put clearly before our eyes the white cathedrals against the blue or gray background of the sky. We must get that image into our hearts. And then we shall be able to continue our reflections.

I wish to show only the great similarity between that past time and the present day. The cathedrals of our own time have not yet been built. The cathedrals belong to other people—to the dead—they are black with grime and worn by centuries. Everything is blackened by soot and eaten away by wear and tear: institutions, education, cities, farms, our lives, our hearts, our thoughts. Nevertheless, everything is potentially new, fresh, in the process of birth. Eyes which are turned away from dead things already are looking forward. The wind is changing; the winter wind gives way to the wind of spring; the sky is still dark with clouds; they are being borne away.

Eyes that see, persons with knowledge, they must be allowed to construct the new world. When the first white cathedrals of the new world are standing, it will be seen and known that they are something true, that something has really begun. With what enthusiasm, what fervor, what relief, the about-face will be made! The proof will be there. Fearful, the world first wants proof.

The proof? The proof, in this country, is that the cathedrals were once white.

When the cathedrals were white, participation was unanimous, in everything. There were no pontificating coteries; the people, the country went ahead. The theater was in the cathedrals, set up on improvised stages in the middle of the nave; they told off the priests and the powerful: the people were grown up and masters of themselves, in the white church—inside and out. "The house of the people," where they discussed mysteries, morality, religion, civil affairs, or intrigues, was entirely white. It was the great expression of liberty of the liberated spirit. The art all around expressed the abundance of thoughts and characters—nature, grossness, eroticism, racy wit, the fear of the spirit in the face of the cosmos, massacres, assassinations, and wars, the pouring out of hearts before God, God Himself, Hermetic thought. As yet there was no Academy to govern everything. People were direct and raw, frank.

At the Court of Miracles—as today in Belleville or Grenelle —at the archbishop's palace or in the house of the prince, people invented the new words of the language. They created a French tongue. The new words expressed a new society.

In the immense hubbub of the Middle Ages which falsely seems to us like a massacre in which blood never stopped flowing, human beings observed the Hermetic rules of Pythagoras; everywhere you could see the eager search for the laws of harmony. They had deliberately turned their backs on "the antique," on the stereotyped models of Byzantium; but they threw themselves passionately into the reconquest of the fatal axis of human destiny: harmony. The law of numbers was transmitted from mouth to mouth among initiates, after the exchange of secret signs.[1]

The Tour Saint-Jacques in Paris is a gigantic rebus worked out on the basis of the cabala. What a profound source of study for anyone willing to risk it! By way of contrast, think of the stupidity of a "Grand Palais" of 1900 in which several Academicians had a chance to speak their message in enormous dimensions!!!

Paris had become the torch of the world. Society was forming, becoming organized, was establishing its broad decrees, liberating itself, building materially and spiritually. Universalism was carried far by the arts and thought, and especially by the active force of a nation which was on its way wholeheartedly, without backward glances, youthfully sustained by the daily creative effort.

The cathedrals were white, thought was clear, spirit was alive, the spectacle clean.

1 Books did not yet exist. These rules of harmony are complicated, delicate. To understand the reason in them you have to have a spirit of some sensibility. Speak of them openly? That would be to put them in danger of errors of fact and of understanding; after three generations they would have become grotesque and the works constructed in accordance with their law would have been caricatures. They must be absolutely exact. From the time books came into being these rules could be set down between two pages and exist intact, accurate and pure. When books became one of the most precious instruments of knowledge, the secret of the rules of harmony no longer had any justification.

From the twenty-fifth to the twenty-eighth of July 1934, the League of Nations, through its International Institute of Intellectual Co-operation, organized in Venice, in a room of the Ducal Palace, an International Conference on Contemporary Arts and Reality, Art and the State.

France had several delegates—(how did it happen that I was one of them?). I jumped, and how! when a thoughtless painter, wishing to make clear what art was, and in what way our period (the modern period) was bankrupt because it is reluctant to buy framed pictures and to use sculpture for its houses, ended his talk by this illuminating remark: "Wearied by their precise civilization, Americans come to France to enjoy the charm of a bandy-legged table!"

Say such a thing—along with a thousand others—over an apéritif at the Deux-Magots: but don't come thus before an international meeting to express the spirit of France!

It is true that this group was composed of historians of art —of past art, but the League of Nations was seeking a line of procedure to illuminate the march of contemporary society. . . .

Supremacy of the "bandy-legged table"! Gentlemen, are we mad? There is no point in going to Venice to turn the Ducal Palace into a padded cell!

I intervened and made Venice a witness—a city which, because of its foundation of water, represents the most formal machinery, the most exact functioning, the most incontrovertible truth—a city which in its unity, unique in the world, still is (because of its foundation of water) a complete and integral image of the harmonized and hierarchic actions of a society.

I am well aware that after the magnificent functioning machine had been fully established "artists" came to Venice. But everything had already been organized, rooted in the place, made by the collaboration of everyone.

Renaissance artists, from that time on, give us the measure of rootlessness. They place themselves above things; they are not so fundamental as those things. Now they are the ones who have been drawn to our attention and who have been imposed upon us in the schools by our instructors. With them life stops; often there results a fair of vanities—a sect setting itself up over society.

But those of us who live intensely in the present moment of modern times, have broken through the boundaries of such limited and poverty-stricken curiosity. We have extended our *sympathy* to all the world and to all times. We have rediscovered life and the axis of all human marvels and agonies. We are far from the theatrical stage which tries to place events of qualitative interest above and outside of human labors. We plunge into daily realities, are face to face with consciousness itself.

We appeal to the reality of the things which make up the life of the world and of each individual person.

We carry out the transmutation of qualitative virtues within the whole active mass, virtues that, through several decadent centuries, a sect believed it could appropriate for itself, and most especially and frightfully, in the past fifty years.

Our task requires the *participation* of everyone, in an orderly way, and not topsy-turvily; hierarchically, and not denatured by artificial doctrines. If Venice, even today, is an intact proof of a collective life, we in France can set up before our eyes the image of the time when the cathedrals were white.

Life bursts forth everywhere, outside the studios where art is "made," outside of the small circles where it is talked about, outside of the writings in which the *spirit of quality* is isolated, localized, and disintegrated.

There is no crisis in life.

There is a crisis only in a corporation: that of the makers of art.

The plastic artists of the world are everywhere in the midst of an intense, multiple, unlimited production. Every day, every hour, the Earth sees splendors surging up which are truths and *present-day* beauty. Ephemeral perhaps! Tomorrow, new truths and new beauties bloom. The day after tomorrow, etc. . . .

Thus life is replenished, full. Life is beautiful! We do not have—do we?—any intention or claim to fix the destiny of the eternal *things of the future?* Everything, at every hour, is only the work of the present moment.

The present moment is creative, creating with an unheard-of intensity.

A great epoch has begun.

A new epoch.

Already manifest in innumerable individual and collective works, forming part of the totality of contemporary production; surging from studios, mills, factories, from the minds of engineers, of artists—objects, laws, projects, thoughts—machine civilization breaks forth.

New times!

It was in every way similar, once, seven centuries ago, when a new world was being born, when the cathedrals were white!

2 DECADENCE OF THE SPIRIT

NEWSPAPERS

One morning at the end of the winter, when I woke up with the painful taste of the pettiness of which life seems to be made, I had a splendid revelation of the felicities of our days, stuffed to the breaking point with stimulating facts. Page after page of my paper burst with life; from headline to headline the arches of imagination made a clear route toward the synthesis of modern conquests. This summary of the news, I tell myself, is an admirable song of hope. Each day brings its harvest. We are unfortunate if we do not see it or know it; we are blind if each morning we fail to discover the promise of new times.

Bent over our narrow labors, subjected like the damned to the rule of money, we no longer know how to see or feel: the world opens up, and every morning brings a new account of it to us, the epic song of the present day. Poetry, heroism, conquest occur every day and everywhere and in everything. The

sublime hammers on the hours. The telegraph has put the palpitation of the world into our hands.

This Monday paper (usually stale since it is made up of
"bottom-drawer material") has, today, forty-eight articles under
headlines.

There are many who read three papers a day—morning,
noon, evening—another way of telling one's beads of uncon-
sciousness in the bus, the subway, or at the family table. It comes
in one ear and goes out the other; quite plainly that wearies the
retina and predisposes one to sleep. The hours pass, the days
pass, life passes. Events are all around us, we do not enter into
them.

Nevertheless, the song of hope is published every day.

MONEY

The stadium of the Parc des Princes in Paris is just outside
my window. On Sunday I endure the noises, cries, whistles, and
shouts of forty thousand spectators. There is a scoreboard at the
south end of the stadium. On its vast, dark surface white letters
are put up, the initials of the teams, and the score. The scoreboard is the crown of a stadium.

There was a clock at the corner of the scoreboard; it is an
indispensable instrument during a game; the clock keeps time
for the players and for the spectators, it controls the nerves of
the crowd, it is connected with the destiny of the players, minute
after minute.

For three days now, the clock has been at 12:30. Because of present-day carelessness the management has not found the fifteen francs necessary to repair the stadium clock. Today, when the management has taken in half a million francs, the clock is not working. Negligence, slackness.

The clock has not been fixed.

The clock isn't there any more! Today it was covered by a poster advertising milk chocolate; two-fifths of the scoreboard proclaim the virtues of a particular shoe polish. Two-fifths of the scoreboard, the crown of the stadium, remain usable. The crown of the stadium has been sold in order to make money. The crown, the part that dominates the stadium. Its dignity, its standing, its morality have been sold to make a few francs. And that in the face of forty thousand paying spectators. In the face of foreign visitors who come here to participate in decisive international jousts, in which France raises its banner beside those of rival countries. A dirty sort of spirit, slovenliness, baseness. France was thoroughly trounced by Holland; the sporting papers call it "the catastrophe of last Sunday." The sporting papers say that a moral crisis is involved; they are well aware of it, in everything. They carry a headline in large type: "A French team without spirit and without a leader." The numbers on the scoreboard were so dirty that I could scarcely read them with my opera glasses. A poor kind of maintenance.

France lost to Switzerland, to Italy, to Spain.

The scoreboard has been sold and in addition the whole stadium is covered with advertisements for apéritifs, oils, or licorice.

I see again the stadiums of American universities. In the USA the welfare of major sports is in the hands of university students. The honor of sport is upheld among all the universities. The whole country takes part in it with an unimaginable fervor. Sixty thousand, a hundred thousand spectators participate at these remarkable jousts, in which everything is conducted with propriety, style, enthusiasm, in gigantic concrete bowls, uncluttered and clean. Love, and a feeling of responsibility. This will give us, a little later in the book, an opportunity to note a trait of character of the country.

The scoreboard sold to shoe polishes! It is a stench in our nostrils, the result of a great illusion which came from America a long time ago during the period of mad "prosperity": make money, make big money! In France books entitled *How to Make Money* were published by travelers who were dazzled by their trip to the country of dollars. America was about to crash. But the example took hold: we are still sucking the last drops of the blood of our country.

SAINT FRONT OF PERIGUEUX

The old church, Saint-Étienne de la Cité, has not been "renovated" or "restored" by the services of the Office of Historic Monuments. That care was reserved for the Church of Saint Front. Both are decisive manifestations of great architecture in the Romanesque-Byzantine style. (Let us note in passing that they did not trouble themselves about nationalist scruples when they sent an abbott to Venice to get the measurements of St. Mark's in order to attempt "to do as much" "here at home." And St. Mark's itself was inspired by the Church of the Holy Apostles in Constantinople. Thought had no frontiers or national boundaries.)

Saint-Étienne, left in its destitution, is admirable and disturbing; Saint Front, violated by restorers, is henceforth lost.

I believe in the *skin* of things, as in that of women.

At Saint Front they have scraped everything, retouched, remade, inch by inch. They have falsified everything: liars, forgers. By what right? Tragic confusion! I know perfectly well that their intentions were good. Alas, alas!

Peril of restorations. Why have they not occupied themselves instead with making new cathedrals, I mean: by looking forward in spirit in place of looking backward so obstinately and weakly, valuing and considering only things that have been lived through.

In Saint Front, on the altars of the church and the stalls of the porch, plaster Gods and Saints reveal a terrible decadence.

The God that you recognize so clearly in traveling through the Near East or North Africa, the man-God that you find there in the midst of crowds: violent, passionate, active (as indeed his Word proclaims him to be in every verse), Jesus, they have made into a bleating pastry.

And they sell God in mass-produced replicas, in all sizes, at all prices, cheaply, so that He may be put on shelves, among the trashy domestic knick-knacks. Idolatry encouraged in order to bring in a few pennies.

To bring in a few pennies, they have falsified the highest ideas.

BORDEAUX STATION

I was on my way to Pessac, a suburb of Bordeaux, to attempt
to unravel the dreadful intrigue which, for six years, immobilized
and tried to reduce to nothing the generous and passionate
undertaking of Henry Frugès.

"I want to show my country"—he had decided—"that a new
period of architecture has come and that with bold methods
and a fresh ethical attitude it is possible to create dwellings which
will bring joy to their users and which answer the needs of a new
consciousness." Fifty-one houses have been constructed at Pessac, in re-enforced concrete, with methods so new . . . that
opinion has been worked up about it.

First the contractors in the region, upset in their routines;
then the architects, who were quite furious. They stirred up
opinion; opinion can be stirred up to an inconceivable degree.
All this would never have happened if Pessac had been built on
the outskirts of Paris, for Parisians do not allow themselves to
be led by the nose so easily. In short, at the Mayor's office, at
the Prefect's office, and at the Water Company they refused to
let the village have any water! That lasted for six years. Two ministers intervened energetically: first M. A. de Monzie, then M.
Loucheur. They made a trip to Pessac. But a village mayor is
stronger than two ministers. And then came ridicule, and written statements, libels and serious reports with the conclusion:
"that the particular character of this architecture made living in
the village impossible and that the residents had all gone away."

The village was empty, all right; it had been for six years
because there was no water. M. Frugès had been martyred. But
his work, praised everywhere abroad, was analyzed in reviews and
daily papers and served as a point of departure for vast enterprises carried through outside of France. The Municipal Council

of Paris sent investigating committees to Germany to gather information while weeds grew up in Pessac.

I was in the Bordeaux station, then, late in the afternoon of
a summer day. The station is disgusting. Not an employee on
the crowded platform. An official with gilded insignia does not
know when the Paris train will arrive. At the office of the station-
master they are evasive, no one knows exactly. General uproar,
offensive filthiness; the floor is black, broken up, the immense
windows are black. At 9:00 P.M. the express stops at platform
No. 4 completely cluttered up with boxes of vegetables, fish,
fruit, hats, screeching fowl, returned empty bags . . . (I noted
down these details on the spot).

. . . In the city, the paving is coming apart. On the Gironde,
the new re-enforced concrete docks are decorated with false pilasters. The preceding year, coming from Buenos Aires, I had disembarked from the *Lutétia* in the midst of an inexpressible confusion. A thousand passengers with all their baggage to pass
through the customs. We have come from far away, we are
being awaited impatiently, hearts are excited. Imagine! Admit-
tance is forbidden to those who have come to meet us. My
mother and my wife are outside, in the rain (Bordeaux rain) in
December; the customs inspection takes place in a miserable new
shed where confusion reigns. A sad spectacle for those returning
from Rio de Janeiro, Santos, Montevideo, Buenos Aires, where
vast installations take care of this very thing: a thousand, two
thousand travelers or emigrants emptied all at once out of the
sides of a large ship. At the office of the French Line in Paris,
where I talked to one of the officials about my idea of having
"air conditioning" on steamships passing from winter to summer
in two weeks after having gone through the two equatorial
tropics, I was told: "Remember, sir, that none of our engineers
has ever made a sea trip! . . ."

Further in, on the Gironde, on both sides of the estuary,
the two orphan pylons of the traveling platform bridge have
been standing for twenty years (perhaps much longer). The

bridge meant to connect the two banks has never been put up. Politics! Yes, it seems that the matter of the bridge is to be voted on. Until there is a new vote, then, there is nothing to do but climb the obstructed banks to the century-old bridge; trucks, cars, and pedestrians add up stupid and expensive miles in going from the left bank docks to the right bank docks—through the heart of the port of Bordeaux, a great city of France which had its white cathedral and which had Colbert and Louis XIV.

Such is the nature of the spirit which exists, today, in many important places of France.

CONDITIONED AIR

My great friend Gustave Lyon died last Sunday at the age of seventy-nine, in full vigor. His corpse was already enclosed in the coffin covered with black cloth, and four candles were burning. His sister said to me: "Now that he has gone, perhaps the value of the great work to which he consecrated his life will be recognized."

With Pleyel Hall—and in spite of the defects of such an ambitious first attempt—he had put the Academy out of architecture. From that time on, no auditorium in the world was planned in accordance with the scheme of the official schools; all of them had to refer to that acoustical and orthophonic lesson.

In that auditorium Gustave Lyon had provided "regulated air" for three thousand auditors. The first accomplishment of the kind in Europe. His studies in providing pure air, which began a long time ago, were independent of the experiments which were made also in the USA. For our Palace of the League of Nations of 1927, we had applied the same method and had combined it with an invention of my own going back to 1916: "neutralizing walls." These walls make it possible to cancel out the cooling effects of the large glazed surfaces characteristic of the new architecture. In 1929, on my return from Moscow, I had established definitively the theory of the "neutralizing wall" and had combined it, in our Centrosoyus Palace (standing today not far from the Kremlin), with the "regulated air" of Gustave Lyon. The combination was called "conditioned air." My friend came to our workshop to see the drawings and models before they were sent to Moscow. "It's an idea of genius," he said, "which transforms all the traditions of the house and of work in residential or business buildings, in studios or factories." Timorous Moscow stuck to current practices and rejected our "conditioned air"; behind our immense sheets of glass they installed radiators, as is customary.

We were looking for an opportunity. It came; the shelter of the Salvation Army, the "City of Refuge." Six hundred poor creatures, men and women, live there. They were given the free and ineffable joy of full light and the sun. A sheet of glass more than one thousand square yards in size lights the rooms from floor to ceiling, and from wall to wall. The director of the shelter told us last week that the joy thus dispensed helped his organization along marvelously, immensely. The sheet of glass was hermetic, since warmed and cleaned air circulated abundantly inside, regulated by the heating plant and the blowers.

The building stood in the sinister Chevaleret quarter. The president of the Republic was to open it in December. In the memory of man it had never been so cold as it was at that moment. Sarcastic comments began to appear in the papers: "What a catastrophe," they predicted, "behind that window which . . . and that . . .'" We went ahead, we opened. It was splendid. The ceremonies took place in the midst of the cold spell in a perfect interior temperature. Two thousand persons are witnesses to it. The manager, Albin Peyron, a virilely optimistic man who has won over the heart of Paris and made of his "army" a liked and respected troop, the manager breathed more easily. It worked!

The City of Paris breathed less easily. The public services were suffocating! What, a vast hermetically sealed building, without openings? That cannot be allowed! The building service of Police Headquarters sent out its architect. He submitted a report to the effect that the system used was irreproachable for the purpose of supplying pure air to guests of doubtful cleanliness. The report gathered dust and for two years the City of Refuge functioned perfectly.

Difficulties did not develop except at the height of the summer, during heat waves.

The small sum of money allotted to the construction had made possible only the functioning of the winter system. The system for the summer (the cooling of the air) remained to be constructed. No new funds! It was necessary to wait.

Then there was a combined attack from the two Prefectures of Paris, that of the Police and that of the Seine. We explained; we resisted. We brought conclusive reports from Prof. Renaud, doctor at the St. Louis Hospital and a pediatric specialist, from Gustave Lyon, and from an engineer associated with the ventilation industry. It was attested that we were right practically and also theoretically. But the official notices became threatening and subject to prompt execution. The local police commissioner was asked to take repressive measures and to close the City of Refuge.

I was not willing to accept the disemboweling of our building, against all common sense. I was bound not to do so. The building was a landmark, a demonstration. Public opinion took up the debate. The Salvation Army Shelter, known in the whole world through the articles of professional journals, was the object of special visits by tourists. We resisted.

But we were defeated, forced to surrender by the new

manager of the "army." It was necessary to throw money out of the window (that is putting it exactly in this case) and open "false windows"—a term recognized as accurate even by those who demanded that genuine crime.

The Prefectures, in their summonses, said that our façades *were not in accordance with the regulations*. And, cynically, they did not mention that the new arrangements provided for the interior, three times per hour, the proper volume of pure air, cleaned and at the right temperature, in every part, however small.

I could go on indefinitely. The City of Paris defeated us. It repudiated the most decisive kind of progress: pure air for the lungs of the city dwellers. But on the thirty-three kilometers of the Paris fortifications it favored the construction of cheap buildings, justly celebrated today because no progressive kind of construction was used and because there are . . . so many things behind all that, and so much money involved, that, up to now, the press has been strangled with graft.

Except for a few well-studied sections it was possible to baptize this new belt of Paris, constructed during the Machine Age, as "the thirty-three kilometers of shame."

I have just come back from America. Since 1928, in that very powerful country, progressive initiatives have become realities, accepted practices for everyone, and rapid developments have made it possible to provide pure and conditioned air in the offices of skyscrapers, in the subways, in the tunnels under the Hudson, in the coaches of the trains, in planes where one may smoke, in small cottages for ordinary citizens. Everywhere! I read with a tourist's curiosity one of the innumerable enamel plates placed beside each window of the newest skyscraper: *Please do not open the windows so as not to disturb the proper functioning of the air conditioning.*

When the cathedrals were white, there were no regulations. The cathedrals were antiregulation.

The spirit of France is not rule-bound except in periods of

lethargy and ossification. Today, when a new world is surging up under the impulse of technical miracles, the officials of the City of Light apply regulations. And soon there will be no light in the City.

NEVERTHELESS, THE MUNICIPAL COUNCIL RESERVES THE RIGHT . . .

A director of the Beaux-Arts in France thought that, for the International Exposition of 1937, it would be a good thing to entrust the planning to the leaders in architecture who are recognized *urbi et orbi*; each one of these leaders would organize a section and would assign the necessary jobs to qualified persons. Thus the Exposition would have been a manifestation of the new times.

But he was defeated by a clever subterfuge.

Public competitions were set up, under the pretext of giving an opportunity to the "young." Classic method of choosing your own favorites behind a reassuring "anonymity." (The competition for the League of Nations Palace at Geneva was a notable example.)

A general manager of the International Exposition of 1937 created a name: *Art and Technique*, and justified it by a clear-sighted, constructive, and optimistic statement. But he was defeated.

In the course of these active preliminaries we had submitted our idea for 1937: *International Exposition of Housing*. Housing, we thought, is the key of the new machine age civilization, a manifestation of the new consciousness. It caused a bit of excitement. A general director of the Beaux-Arts accepted our proposition and asked us to make it concrete.—"Give us enough ground to set up a 'housing unit'; in a 'unit' all the problems can be made clear: city planning, industrialization of building construction, search for standards, application of new techniques —acoustics, heating, orientation, etc.;—plastic character, general esthetics, the ethic of the dwelling and of the city. A unit will accommodate four thousand people. For the sake of the Exposition, everything will be instructive, didactic. Visitors will see the various unfinished and successive stages of construction: a real lesson in architectural biology. Also, they will see furnished apartments and the community organizations which, some day, are to transform domestic economy by lightening its tasks. We shall put our enterprise under the aegis of the CIAM (International Congress of Modern Architecture, established at Sarraz in 1928 following the scandal about the architectural judgment of the designs for the League of Nations Palace at Geneva). In it the Congress will develop particularly the results of its work on 'The Functional City,' collective labors made by the national groups of eighteen countries, representing a unique documentation, a veritable treasure chest of all the researches made in the interest of improving cities."

We were given the Kellermann bastion on the ring of fortifications of Napoleon III, south of Paris, east of and adjoining University City.

Everything had been discussed, granted, fixed, and adopted by the general director of the Beaux-Arts, the minister of Commerce, the prefect of the Seine, and after stormy debates, by the Municipal Council of Paris, then by the Government. The matter was settled between March and July, 1934.

The finished project to be installed on the allotted ground intended a renovation in the matter of housing, lots, and streets. Because of a clear feeling of the poetry of things, it preserved completely the Kellermann bastion, the sole and unique vestige still remaining of the thirty-three kilometers of the military zone of the Second Empire which was forever destroyed by the Low Cost Housing Project of the City of Paris: a magnificent relic of architecture and of history.

After eighteen months, in September of 1935, M. Marzloff, director of the architectural services of the City of Paris, told me in the presence of two witnesses—Fernand Léger, delegate of the Modern Painters and Sculptors, and René Herbst, delegate of the Union of Modern Artists, two groups which we had brought into our enterprise: "Don't allow yourselves any illusions; you have irreconcilable enemies in the Municipal Council. Did not the president, M. Contenot, say publicly that you are anti-French and that you worked against France at the International Exposition of City Planning in Berlin [where we showed the "radiant city" with a manifesto on a red, white, and blue poster, signed by French artists known throughout the world, but independent of the Academies]? A phrase that the Municipal Council had inserted in the text of the law granting us the ground, the year before at Pentecost, was put there *to prevent you from carrying through your project. . . ."

This is the tiny phrase: *"Nevertheless, the Municipal Council reserves the right eventually to demand the demolition of the buildings constructed on the Kellermann bastion, after the Exposition. . . ."*

For eighteen months the project had been studied, estimates made, the first steps taken for the participation of heavy industry, an international committee called together (CIRPAC, steering committee of the CIAM). For the City of Paris, M. Marzloff had asked us to submit all the details, the program, the methods, the financing, etc. . . ; the principal architects of the Exposition, MM. Letrosne & Greber, had said: "We are making your project ours."

The general director of the Beaux-Arts, the minister, the

prefect, the Government, all that did not count any longer, after the insertion of the little phrase.

Thus the Kellermann bastion got rid of our presence and the Exposition of 1937 likewise.

The municipal administration began to demolish the bastion. That immense bank of earth, a true belvedere, has been razed. The walls of Napoleon III no longer exist. Today it is a formless wasteland "good for building operations," the last link of the thirty-three kilometers of the chain around Paris, in which business transactions satisfactory to many have taken place. Many people were made fools of by the little phrase.

A banana peel under the feet of courageous seekers, slipped there by people well versed in business intrigues. They threw the monkey wrench into the complex machinery of institutional life, including even that of the Government: an edifying sign.

(I shall be much criticized for this chapter and accused of being an ill-bred polemicist. Our disappointment, our broken hopes, the extensive collaboration of the best creative artists of all countries brought together by the Congress under the direction of the French Group—all that is nothing! What is more, they expect us to say thank you!)

GREATNESS IS IN THE INTENTION

In crossing the Franco-Belgian border, the train passes through the mining country. What is that, a mirage? Gigantic pyramids rising from the plains are silhouetted against the sky all the way to the horizon. I am speaking of my first trip, made long ago. My emotion was intense. These sublime monuments sunk into the blue depths, on the left, on the right of the train. They were simply the heaps of slag from the coal mines, piles of gray-black schist, wastes, which once enclosed veins of coal. Now, I understand, the tracks supported on the side of each slope carry the cars to the top of the pyramid where they are dumped. The law of landslides fixes forever the destiny of the pyramids: an impeccable slope of forty-five degrees. And thus I am near Cairo, in the land of the Pharaohs.

No, not at all! My emotion, though still strong, is becoming dulled. My admiration dissolves. Those are not masterpieces, they are not works of art. They are simply schist wastes. And at once I measure the abyss which opens up between the aspect of a thing and the quality of spirit which has brought it into being. The intention is what touches the deepest recesses of our heart, the quality of the spirit brought to the creation of the work of art. Here there is nothing more than an industrial enterprise in which no elevated intention is involved. For good reason! And however fresh my understanding may be, however innocent my heart may be, well, I do not sense here the utterance of a man or of men. It is only a fact and a law of physics. The only emotion which remains is the rigor of that law. Without anything further.

But a debate begins inside me: suppose men had made that; purposefully, to raise our hearts by that intention?

The train has passed through the mining country and the pyramids no longer occupy my thoughts.

In the prologue of the account of this first trip to the USA, under the sign of the white cathedrals, I feel that everything that I shall say will be qualified by the degree and the quality of the intention which has established the skyscraper, set up cities thrusting into the sky, thrown highways across the country, built bridges over estuaries or rivers. Our heart calls to other hearts. That is the measure of our emotion, and magnitude can be depressing, and the schist pyramids can leave us contrite. Greatness is in the intention; and not in dimensions.

When the cathedrals were white, the whole universe was raised up by an immense faith in the energy, the future, and the harmonious creation of a civilization.

PART TWO

U. S. A.

About three years after the year 1000 the churches were renovated throughout the universe, especially in Italy and Gaul, though most of them were still beautiful enough not to require repairs. But the Christian peoples seemed to rival one another in magnificence, raising splendid churches in mutual emulation.

One would have said that the whole world, in a common accord, had shaken off the rags of its past in order to put on a white robe of churches.

CHRONICLE OF RAOUL GLABER,
BENEDICTINE MONK OF BURGUNDY WHO DIED IN 1050.

1   CITIES OF THE WORLD

INVESTIGATOR OF THE SITUATION

Already I have spoken to some hundred thousand people in the world and I have interested them all in a dream. My feet were on the ground, only my glance passed above tumults and confusions. I have become acquainted with cities by having visited, examined, and explored them. I have heard explanations, complaints, expressions of discouragement. Everywhere they told me: "There is no hope of improving things, you have to adapt yourself as best you can to the . . . evil."

What I have been able to say has been of a general character, of principles, doctrinaire if you wish. I have been able also to suggest the particular surgical operation which would set aside a decadent past and open the door to the new times.

My life, by its active adventurousness and by the nature of my character and origins, allows me to get close to ideas brought into relation with the steadiness of the general human scheme, without the obstruction of a too marked regionalism. In the course of years, I have felt myself become more and more a man of everywhere with, nevertheless, one strong root: the Mediterranean, queen of forms under the play of light; I am dominated by the imperatives of harmony, beauty, plasticity. There is in my background a permanent fact: liberty of thought and lack of interest in material gains; freedom in thinking normally conducted above the level of passing events.

In this book, which will be only a declaration, but throughout which I hope to be able to evoke the movement of our violent times, I shall do my best to avoid the conceptions "France," "Germany," "America," "USSR," etc. . . . These conceptions may imply nobility, greatness, love: the love of what one knows, of what one may see and take hold of, of what one is, or better, of what one should be. Conceptions which are profoundly natural if they are the expression of the sense of family, within all the vast limits to which it is susceptible. But conceptions which become depraved and swallowed up in guns and bayonets from the moment that the frontier, which should be imponderable, or at least supple and mobile, becomes the line of demarcation, of separation, the point of divergence, the locale of conflicts, the cunning instrument, precise as a commutator, which infallibly sets off the explosion and assures wars. Natural and noble conceptions or perfidious conceptions covering a mass of sordid, cruel, private interests, manipulating hypocrisy in a frightful way. I feel that danger; I see in it the possibility of maintaining and increasing still more the buttresses of the egoistic "I," of vanity, of property conceived in a narrow and avaricious way, of patrimony artificially organized against the very precepts of nature; nature ends a life, an admirable activity, by death; and nothing is transmissible except the nobility of the fruit of work: thought. Everything else disappears: the immense attainment of an individual during his lifetime. Everything dissolves, everything has to be begun again by each individual person: struggle, effort within one's self, individual, passionate, and yet disinterested

conquest. That is the law of life: death. And that is beautiful,
sublime, for there is no purpose in an egoistic hoarding of treasure. And here is the sad part of it: this noble path has been lit-
tered with bank notes. The stages have been marked by bank
accounts. Money has piled up. And when the great hour comes
—death: "corpse, carcase henceforth useless go to the family
vault or to the crematory. The will, which saves everything, is
in the safe-deposit box; money is transmissible." I really believe
that this is one of the most tragic weaknesses by which men have
allowed themselves to be enslaved.

This egoism, extended from the individual case to the collective case, has set nation against nation, injured and paralyzed
civilization, and it weakens our efforts today. Today more than
ever, infinitely more, ridiculously more, thought is rigged out
in a uniform whose belt is too tight. What existed formerly—in
the time of "universal" civilizations, for there were no barriers
—the law of the sun, the law of the flow of water and the law
of undecipherable destinies, has become police record material:
first of all, nationality. And according as interests are now hostile, now favorable, judgment is black or white. Thus are established the barriers hampering the natural movement of human
works, which develop in accordance with unfathomable causes
on the earthly sphere where everything is (and should be) continuous, contiguous, interpenetrating, extensible, "sympathetic"
and not antipathetic.

Listen carefully, for example, to the "elevated" discussions
organized on the occasion of the centenary celebrations for
Goethe at Frankfurt by the International Institute of Intellectual Co-operation, an agency of The League of Nations: the
Englishman proclaims the name of Shakespeare; the Frenchman
that of Rabelais or Balzac; the Italian replies with Dante and
Michelangelo, the Spaniard with Cervantes. Though each one
points to his own flag, in passing Goethe receives a considerable
share of compliments (and sometimes these dithyrambs have
a comic sound, the speaker making it clear that he understands

everything about the greatness of Goethe and that he has something of it himself). They are busy with bickerings and squab-
bles! But agreement exists about Mahomet, for he is of a country
which does not yet have a delegation at this court of high culture; he does not belong to one of the nations "involved," he is
outside of the "I's" and the "me's" which appear at every turn
in the discussion.

When the cathedrals were white, above nationalities concerned with themselves, there was a common idea: Christendom
was above everything else. Already, before constructing everywhere the naves of the new civilization, a common enthusiasm
of spirit had brought together the peoples of modern times and
had led them, through strange avatars, toward Jerusalem, where
there was the seat of a universal thought: love.

So I should wish to be nothing more than one of those
who seek to discern the "constructive" paths, to prepare "tomorrow"; who observe good with sympathy, evil coolly, and who,
above all, allow themselves to be led toward something useful,
guided by their nose—that subtle apparatus of scent that the
gods have put as a promontory on our faces to enable us to use
the forces accumulated by instinct—instinct being the individual
"gift" that destiny has given us as well as the sum of innumerable
conscious and unconscious experiences stored up by a vigilant
spirit.

MOTIVE OF MY JOURNEY

The third day after my arrival in America, I was asked to make a statement from Radio City, to be broadcast over fifty stations in the USA. Radio City is a machine age temple installed in one of the skyscrapers of Rockefeller Center.

The temple is solemn, surfaced with somber marble, shining with clear mirrors mounted in stainless steel frames. Silence. Corridors and vast spaces; doors open automatically: they are the silent elevators unloading passengers. No windows anywhere. . . . Silent walls. "Conditioned" air throughout, pure, clean, at a constant temperature. Am I on the fifth floor or the fortieth? The broadcasting studios are large, impeccable; they close your mouth before you think of opening it. In each room spectators occupy an amphitheater which is outside of it, enclosed as if they were in a glass aquarium. They are free to speak; none of their chatter escapes the aquarium. What do they see? An orchestra, a singer; in this case, a gentleman with glasses who affably greets the charming Mrs. Claudine MacDonald. What do they hear? The slightest sound emitted, transmitted by a loudspeaker. The spectacle amuses them, since the amphitheater is full. The gentleman is seated at a table with a pitcher of ice water and paper cups. Everyone is at his post. The instruments, moving in their mysteriousness, and the technician in charge, are in another quite small aquarium. The clock is dictator. When I was finished, I was sent into the little aquarium where one may talk. It was then that an object attracted my attention; recognizing what it was, I pointed out to my companion, Fernand Léger, a straight red needle turning around a dial marked 1 to 60. They are seconds. The needle is obsessing; I said to Léger, "Notice the needle that goes around so fast: it marks the seconds and nothing else. The clock beside it marks the hours. Small matter! The hours will return tomorrow. But the dial with the second hand is something cosmic, it is time itself, which never returns. That red needle is a material evidence of the movement of worlds."

In my radio speech I said: "With the simplicity of a professional who has dedicated his life to the study of the first cycle of the machine age, I bring into the domain of architecture and city planning propositions which call into service all the techniques of modern times, but whose final aim is to go beyond simple utility. The indispensable purpose is to give to the men of the machine age the joys of the heart and of health.

"Such a plan is neither European nor American. It is human and universal. It represents an urgent task. We must replace the brutality of the present, the misery and stupidity, by what I have called 'the essential joys.'

"A hundred years have been enough to make cities inhuman.

"Monday morning, when my ship stopped at Quarantine, I saw a fantastic, almost mystic city rising up in the mist. But the ship moves forward and the apparition is transformed into an image of incredible brutality and savagery. Here is certainly the most prominent manifestation of the power of modern times. This brutality and this savagery do not displease me. It is thus that great enterprises begin: by strength.

"In the evening, on the avenues of the city, I began to appreciate the people who, by a law of life which is their own, have been able to create a race: handsome men, very beautiful women.

"The world is undergoing one of the great metamorphoses of history. The collective and the individual collide instead of combining. Is a synthesis possible? Yes, in a program on a *human scale* and guided by *human wisdom*.

"This is architecture's hour. There can be no new architecture without a new city planning. New cities have always replaced old cities, by periods. But today it is possible for the city of modern times, the happy city, the radiant city, to be born.

"The architecture of the academies is superannuated. Architecture rejoins its destiny, which is *the setting in order of the present time*. Let's not talk any longer about styles, either modern or ancient; *the style is the event itself*. Machine age society will make itself manifest in its thought, in its instruments of production, and in its physical machinery: *houses and cities*, expressions of the aspirations of a modern consciousness. *That is where style is!*

"America, which is in a process of permanent evolution, which possesses infinite reserves of materials, which is animated by an energy potential unique in the world, is surely the country first able to bring to fulfillment, and with an exceptional perfection, this contemporary task.

"I believe within myself that the ideas that I bring here and that I present under the phrase 'radiant city,' will find in this country their natural ground. In coming to explain this first doctrine for equipping machine civilization, these constructive, optimistic and active theses, bold ones perhaps, but full of faith in the power of modern times, I am certain to secure the adhesion of those whose experience and personal judgment have led to the same hopes."

Rio de Janeiro, capital of Brazil, led the way. In 1936, I was asked, with Lucio Costa's enthusiastic group, to study anew the plans for the Education and Health Building and to make the first suggestions for the University City of Brazil. I brought the "sun-breaker" to the tropics, the building supported on posts, the wall of glass, the roof garden. . . . War came! . . . Liberation of Paris, 1944; then I learned what they had built in Rio, and in Recife, and in Pampulha. And that a skyscraper of the new type is now in existence, rational and smiling, fit to serve modern work.

NEW YORK, A VERTICAL CITY

New York is a vertical city, under the sign of the new times. It is a catastrophe with which a too hasty destiny has overwhelmed courageous and confident people, though a beautiful and worthy catastrophe. Nothing is lost. Faced with difficulties, New York falters. Still streaming with sweat from its exertions, wiping off its forehead, it sees what it has done and suddenly realizes: "Well, we didn't get it done properly. Let's start over again!" New York has such courage and enthusiasm that everything can be begun again, sent back to the building yard and made into something still greater, something mastered! These people are not on the point of going to sleep. In reality, the city is hardly more than twenty years old, that is the city which I am talking about, the city which is vertical and on the scale of the new times.

Morocco, which is contemporary with New York, is not under the sign of the new times. France established itself in the midst of a drowsy Moslem civilization. The evidences of brilliant moments sleep in the sun: in Fez, a superb city, and everywhere in the country, there are mosques, palaces of sultans and caliphs, markets still vibrating with life. They are a disillusioned race, but magnificent, noble, under the sign of dignity. France has been able to accomplish various things: she brought well-being, education, and above all loyalty and justice. Benefits which were somewhat imposed but which must be considered the indispensable signs of civilization. The army—an army of "professional" soldiers—was the authority. They furrowed the country with a magnificent network of roads of the French type. And cities were raised. Alas, they were behind the times, questions were unsolved. We always live under the burden of current ideas. While New York was rising into the air, London and the towns of Germany were satisfied with the illusory idea of garden cities: a rural humanity, living idyllically in cottages, served daily by a purgatory of transportation systems. Every day they sank more deeply into the paradox. And New York also, and likewise Chicago, since that was the fashion, at the very moment when a vague feeling drove them to set up, straight and inflexible in the sky, the first landmarks of the new times. Thus France believed that she was doing the right thing: charming villages were set up for the admiration of the old and splendid Arab civilization, beneath the tutelary shadow of a modern army.

I believe that cities animated by the new spirit, ordered in an even grander way—infinitely grander—than those formerly erected by Louis XIV or Napoleon, constructed of steel and glass, standing erect beside the sea, or standing erect in the valleys or on the plateau at the foot of the Atlas Mountains, would have created among the Arabs an atmosphere of enthusiasm, of admiration, of respect, through the remarkable means at the disposal of architecture and city planning. In them the Arab would have found a teacher, a guide. No longer would he have raised his eyebrows in doubt. Both hands held out, abandoning from that moment all futile dissembling, he would have loved, admired, understood the new times, and respected France with all his conviction. Architecture and city planning can be great educators.

France wished to be charming. Its reputation is to be charming. Americans think that we are charming relations. They are not afraid of us, they are delighted by our company. When the cathedrals were white, the journeymen masons paid no attention to being charming. They had built and they were building structures of the greatest dignity in a burst of tension, energy, tenacity, and fidelity to a great idea. When they sculptured the porches or the capitals of Autun, of Moissac, of Vézelay or of Angoulême, the journeymen stonecutters were not concerned about being dainty. The harsh destiny of men struggling with the elements or the unfathomable unknown led their hearts and hands toward robust, indeed tragic feelings. The times were strong. They were new times. They were building a world. And they were as much the less barbarous or primitive as the architecture was bold, a tangible sign of knowledge, of strength, of mastery in movement, increasing, in a process of becoming. Thus the leaderships are inscribed in the stone rising in the sky and in the power of the techniques. A unanimous feeling lifts up their enterprises: they believe.

For twenty years also, Buenos Aires, in an oppressive tumult, has been lifted up by the spirit of the times. When order is in control, that city will become one of the great places of the world.

And here are still other combinations: Moscow struggling with the dilemma of an inadequate technique and contradictory ideas; Barcelona, shaken by revolutionary eruptions, a city geographically dedicated to a new destiny. Rome, weighed down under an artificial *décor* by a resurrection (of dubious value) of its past, hesitates instead of speaking out with certitude. Finally Algiers, the capital of North Africa, a young colony which is inclined to courageous action, is held back by its city councillors and is uneasy about being the first to risk the adventure of the new times.

Where on the varied earth, in the whirlwind of innumerable conflicts, shall the young people of today go to breathe the air of the new times? There can be no doubt: a crust is scaling off of our stupefied societies. New skin! Spring! Renewal! The young are eager for a change of air. I feel myself young also; I have the desire, before dying, to share in something live and changing. I do not wish to be charming, but to be strong. I do not wish to be frozen, I do not wish to maintain things, but to act and create.

I cannot forget New York, a vertical city, now that I have had the happiness of seeing it there, raised up in the sky.

"I AM AN AMERICAN!"

"Like us, like Americans, my friend. You can like them, they deserve to be liked. This is a country in which there is a great deal of confusion, a great deal of activity, a great deal going on, a country in which everything is open and everything is possible. Look at New York raised up around us, carrying up to hitherto inaccessible heights a vertical city. It is natural that your spirit should often protest. Well and good! But with your heart you can understand us; with your heart you can feel that we are young, a little mad, or rather children, and that we love work and great things; and that we know nothing of discouragements. We possess a great country which has made us great; at least it has made our undertakings great. We are strong. We are driving ahead; everything is changing here; events take place in days; with you it is in centuries! Everything is changing, everything is being transformed; tomorrow will be different. We have a prodigious potential. When we shall have found our way, we shall do things that will please you.

"Come back to America, my friend, America is a great country."

A woman spoke to me thus, on my last evening in New York. My heart was a little torn by the imminent departure, a heart which had been torn every day for two months by hate and love of this new world which must be seen to be really known as it is. Hate or love: nothing more, nothing less. Daily debate. Better, debate through every minute in the midst of the stupefying city. Hours of despair in the violence of the city (New York or Chicago); hours of enthusiasm, confidence, optimism, in the fairy splendor of the city.

I am not able to bear the thought of millions of people undergoing the diminution of life imposed by devouring distances, the subways filled with uproar, the wastelands on the edges of the city, in the blackened brick streets, hard, implacably soulless streets—tenement streets, streets of hovels that make up the cities of the century of money—the slums of New York or Chicago.

I am offended by this blow at legitimate human hopes. Nevertheless, if I am observant, I discover that my despair is not always shared by the victims themselves. In New York, the people who have come in order to "make money" shake off black thoughts and, looking at the sparkle of the great avenues, the entrances of apartment houses and fine homes, think: "O.K., it will be my turn tomorrow!"

Seven million people are bound in the chains of New York, and that turn will never come unless they learn to adopt drastic measures.

Knowing quite well that that turn cannot come quickly enough for seven million beings, there are moments when I hate the city of today; clearly and coolly I know that a proper plan can make New York the city par excellence of modern times,

can actively spread daily happiness for these oppressed families
—children, women, men stupefied by work, stunned by the noise
of the rails of the subways or elevateds—who sink down each
evening, at the end of their appointed tasks, in the impasse of
an inhuman hovel.

In sober offices, on the fifty-sixth floor of the newest skyscraper, men carry on business. Big business probably. I do not
have a sense of figures and I know from experience that it is
often more difficult to make small matters come out right than
big ones. In the domain of money, the law is like that of the
swing at the fair: at the beginning the effort is normal; everyone can take off and make a start. But at a certain point in the
swing, when the acrobat is on the horizontal, it becomes precarious; he is too far away from the gravitational norm, and
gravity acts on him. Then it takes an effort of a very particular
kind to achieve a vertical position, with head down, and having
passed the "meridian" of the swing, to come on around effort-
lessly from that point. Brute strength is not enough. The repeated attempts require a regular and harmonious progression.
Harmonious, that's the word. Harmony is the cause of the success. The most difficult thing—the real difficulty—comes when
you are a hair's-breadth from success: at the moment of swing-
ing over. If you manage it, you are thenceforth launched! Many
will not succeed in managing it. Those who have passed over this
financial hazard owe it to their merits just as they owe it to the
combination of circumstances: the things necessary to make the
effort profitable, to stimulate it, to support it, were present. It
was a happy conjuncture. And now the financial swing moves
easily, with no further effort required except a scrupulous supervision.

That is why the skyscrapers were not constructed with a
wise and serious intention. They were applauded acrobatic feats.
The *skyscraper as proclamation* won. Here the skyscraper is not
an element in city planning, but a banner in the sky, a fireworks

rocket, an aigrette in the coiffure of a name henceforth listed in the financial Almanach de Gotha.

Beneath the immaculate office on the fifty-sixth floor the vast nocturnal festival of New York spreads out. No one can imagine it who has not seen it. It is a titanic mineral display, a prismatic stratification shot through with an infinite number of lights, from top to bottom, in depth, in a violent silhouette like a fever chart beside a sick bed. A diamond, incalculable diamonds.

The great masters of economic destiny are up there, like eagles, in the silence of their eminences. Seated in their chairs, framed by two plate glass windows which fuse their rooms with the surrounding space, they appear to us made out of the substance of this event which is as strong and violent as a cosmic mutation: New York standing up above Manhattan is like a rose-colored stone in the blue of a maritime sky; New York at night is like a limitless cluster of jewels. America is not small potatoes! In the last twenty years, facing the old continent, it has set up the Jacob's ladder of the new times. It is a blow in the stomach that strikes you like a hurricane.

"I am an American."

"It was not they who said it. I thought it for them.

How dare you curse New York? "Fairy catastrophe" (I shall return to that theme), unified splendor, scintillation, promise, proof, act of faith (what faith?), etc.

It is the first time that men have projected all their strength and labor into the sky—a whole city in the free air of the sky. Good God, what disorder, what impetuosity! What perfection already, what promises! What unity in a molecular state, gridiron street plan, office on top of office, clear crystallization. It is sublime and atrocious, and nothing succeeds any longer. There is nothing to do except to see clearly, think, conceive, begin over again. Of course New York is ready to begin over again. Those people have courage!

That afternoon I had gone through the Holland Tunnel

to the other side of the Hudson and over the Skyway, an elevated road so named because it rises on piles or arches high above industrial areas, arms of the sea, railways and roads, over an immense expanse. A road without art because no thought was given to it, but a wonderful tool. The "Skyway" rises up over the plain and leads to the "skyscrapers." Coming from the flat meadows of New Jersey, suddenly it reveals the City of the Incredible Towers.

I shall come back to America. America is a great country. Hopeless cities and cities of hope at the same time. What an idea of the action between these two poles is thus expressed, what a battlefield is spread out between these two feelings which exist in the gasping heart of every man of action, of every man who believes enough in something to dare to attempt it, and who risks catastrophe for having wished to bring back trophies to the altar.

For, beyond the narrow limits of the average in human things, when magnitude enters into an undertaking (Assyrians, Hindus, Egyptians, Romans, and Gothic builders), the result becomes a public and civic thing and, like grace, makes a horror sublime.

All the French people whom I met on the ship going to New York, all those on this ship taking us back to Paris, resolve the question thus: "Once you have opened the door on America you cannot close it again."

NEW YORK IS NOT A COMPLETED CITY . . .

It is a city in the process of becoming. Today it belongs to the world. Without anyone expecting it, it has become the jewel in the crown of universal cities in which there are dead cities whose memories and foundations alone remain and whose evocation is exalting; in which there are living cities injured by the narrow mold of past civilizations. Here is nobility, grandeur of outlines. Here are expressive, animated, proud topographies, exciting landscapes. Here are the old wisdoms accumulated century after century, harmoniously joined together by the simple passage of years, although everything in it has been contrasts, contradictions, revolutionary progress in techniques and conceptions. Here is Paris, for example, jumbled, yet with a gracious harmony: vertical Gothic, pure rectilinear Renaissance, pure *Grand Siècle* horizontal, strong Louis XV, elegant and sober Louis XVI, square Napoleon, Eiffel filigree. Crown of noble cities, soft pearls, or glittering topazes, or radiant lapis, or melancholy amethysts! New York is a great diamond, hard and dry, sparkling, triumphant.

Suddenly New York has entered the family of the cities of the world, and not by the back door. The American is a Janus: one face absorbed by the anxieties of adolescence, looking toward the troubles of his consciousness; the other face as solid as an Olympic victor's, looking toward an old world which at certain moments he believes he can dominate. Reverse the situation: imagine in an urban drawing room a slightly awkward young man, sympathetic and hard-working, who has come a long way and who causes many well-established people to smile. One day his book, his speech, the battle he has won, explodes in the face of the world. He dominates. Look at his eyes: a hard flame of pride shines in them! Will he become an ass or a king?

New York is not a finished or completed city. It gushes up. On my next trip it will be different. Those of us who have visited it are asked this question: "When you were there in 1939, or in 1928, or in 1926, or in 1920, was such and such already there? Oh, really, you don't know then what an effect that makes!" Such is the rhythm of the city.

The architects rush in with their heads down; after having worked over the "styles" firmly and worthily, they are launched on the paths of the modern spirit. How are they getting along? Badly, very badly, and nevertheless there are successes. Detail, that is all trash! *Style* is developing without them, outside of them, by the result itself, by the formidable internal pressure which mobilizes their efforts. These debatable results, strange, amusing, or striking, are being worked out in the sky. A thousand feet of height is the rule in this frightening type of football. Well then! A thousand feet of height, in stone, steel and glass, standing up in the magnificently blue sky of New York, is a new event in human history which up to now had only a legend on that theme: that of the Tower of Babel.

A thousand feet of height looked at from the streets, or appearing as an ineffable spectacle from the plains of New Jersey, above the Palisades—the cliffs along the Hudson River—that is the scale of the new times.

At present, it is like a house-moving, all the furniture in confusion, scattered about, unkempt. But order will come.

And the express elevators take forty-five seconds to go from the bottom to the top, that is, for sixty-five stories, a time equal to that taken by our elevators, sanctimoniously installed in the Haussmann stair wells, to go to the sixth story.

IT IS A SAVAGE CITY!

Yes. But the men and women are clean and healthy.

Cleanliness is a national virtue in America. No filth, no dust. Sea breezes incessantly sweep through the limpid maritime sky. The offices are clean; the bath tubs, the shops, the glistening hotels; the dazzling restaurants and bars. The immaculate personnel, in shirt sleeves, is shining white. Food is wrapped up in bright cellophane. There is no more real dust than there is symbolic dust, everything is new and spotless, including the collegiate Gothic of the universities.

Paris bistro, you disappointed me on my return, with your faded charm. It's too old, too old, saddening! Not even a nice little old, something neat and clean!

In contrast, there is a style, a true style, in American cleanliness.

People who wash their shirts, paint their houses, clean the glass in their windows, have an ethic different from those who cultivate dust and filth. To prove that they possess an age-old culture, the latter preserve the cracks in the walls, the patina, and what is worse, they have even established the taste for patina, the love of the old, and because of that they hammer out modern "wrought iron" and soil the new wainscoting of their apartments with bistre.

A true culture manifests itself in fresh color, white linen, and clean art. Among the Cyclades of Greece, in the islands where a volcanic topography has prevented the introduction of the wheel—cart, bicycle, car—where transportation is possible only by mule-back; where consequently customs have remained millenary; where you still seem to recognize Agamemnon or Ulysses in the villages, the tradition of a living culture demands that, each Saturday, the joints of the stones forming the steps of the

house and those of the flagstones in front of the house, be painted
with bright whitewash—a radiant filigree. Thus in the Islands
each Sunday begins in cleanliness and whiteness; life is magni-
fied by this testimony: be clean. Go through beautiful France
in a car and you will see that this fundamental feeling of life,
always renewed or renewable, has died down; that cracked walls,
dirt, and negligence are masters of our spirits . . . except here and
there, where there is still faith in the virtue of each hour.

THE STREETS ARE AT RIGHT ANGLES TO
EACH OTHER AND THE MIND IS LIBERATED

Your mind is free instead of being given over every minute
to the complicated game imposed on it by the puzzle of our
European cities. Do you want to go from your home to the
Opera, to Père-Lachaise, to the Luxembourg Museum, or to the
Eiffel Tower? First get the city plan out of your drawer and
look for the route. It is a task. Old gentlemen will pretend to
discover in that the charm of Paris. I do not agree; nevertheless
I accept the inconvenience imposed by the very history of the
city; on my way I thank Louis XIV, Napoleon, and Haussmann
for having cut through the city with some clear and intelligent
axes.

Manhattan, in New York, is a granite rock more than twelve
miles long and two miles wide, between the Hudson River and
the East River. In length it is laid out in nine parallel avenues;
across, in nearly two hundred streets parallel to each other and
at right angles to the avenues. The avenue in the middle, Fifth

Avenue, serves as a spinal column for this gigantic sole. On one side it is west, on the other east. The first street is at the south, on the ocean side, the last is at the north, on the land side. Everything is ordered accordingly. You have to go to 135 East 42nd Street? Everything is determined with a Euclidean clearness. 42nd Street? You are at your hotel on 55th Street; you go to Fifth Avenue, go down thirteen streets. East? You turn left. 135? You walk to number 135. Thus you know instantly whether to walk, whether to take a taxi, or whether to catch the bus on the avenue or use the subway. I say that it is an immense and beneficent freedom for the mind. It will be said that I am stopping over an anatomical detail of the city and that I attach a great deal of importance to it. This is not an anatomical detail, but the outstanding and essential biological structure of the city. It is a question of a fundamental principle. Do you wish the proof of our own vagaries? This grille of streets, this "American layout," is precisely the excuse for the attacks of academicians and romantics. It is our particular vanity to be plunged in disorder down to the very base. We make a virtue of it; we affirm that it is life, rich, subtle, agreeable, and what not! Now the Romans laid out their cities in "the American way"; and the Greeks before them. The Egyptians also. And the French, in the time of the white cathedrals, when new cities were being born—the towns of the South in particular—planned in "the American way." Thus Saint Louis had Aigues Mortes executed, in one building campaign, in "the American way."

When the conquistadors left on caravels for the New World, they took along geometers with plans for cities conceived in advance, laid out in "the American way": the Spanish cuadra is one hundred ten square meters, the cuadra that you see everywhere from a plane, from Buenos Aires, going north, to Montevideo, to Ascension in Paraguay, in the immense pampas, as in the savanna of North America.

Are the Americans then the founders of civilization through the ages? Such is the conclusion to which you lead us, exiles

of our own day, lost in the underbrush of romantic garden cities!
One man sowed that foolish idea. He was an intelligent and
sensitive Viennese, Camillo Sitte, who, quite simply, posed the
problem badly. In travels of discovery through Italy, in medieval
cities strategically placed on hills and tightly encircled by military walls, he was won over by the art which so exactly adjusted
house to house and palace to church—each stone of each city,
a living and subtle plastic character, a spectacle of quality. The
existence of these exquisite things, and on the other hand, the
vast vulgarities of the second half of the nineteenth century,
dedicated to great railroad projects, which brought about the
dreary, sinister, and soulless expanses of the great modern cities:
Vienna, Berlin, Munich, Budapest, etc. . . . On the basis of the
urban horrors of 1870 he concluded his reasoning and declared:
Confusion is beautiful, and rectitude is base. And because on a
small scale, in small Italian towns—Orvieto, Siena, Perugia, etc.
—the walls hung on the sides of hills, the uneven levels of the
ground, pocket-sized open spaces bowed the streets under their
yoke to allow a greater number of houses to pile up like the
scales of a pineapple, he concluded that the beautiful was curved
and that large cities should be contorted. The fashion was
launched: Berlin and Vienna and Munich, and cities throughout
the world, developed curves, became entangled in a net like
that which a cat makes out of a skein of wool. The garden cities
near London, idem, etc. . . . Morocco was constructed in a
crooked way, since straightness was considered an enemy of the
heart! One day in a committee meeting, M. Louis Bonnier, head
architect of the City of Paris, who loves cathedrals and many
excellent things, apostrophized a bewildered young architect in
connection with his city plan project for Saint Raphael: "What
is this, sir, this completely straight two-hundred-meter 'artillery
range'? We shall not allow that to be executed!"

The ten main avenues of New York are nearly fifteen kilometers long. Such are the minds of the same epoch: one saying
gee, another haw!

Fifteen kilometers long? Is it imaginable, is it allowable! Traditions, which have become academized, demand that every straight avenue terminate in a blaze of glory, or if you prefer, in a set piece: the Opera at the end of the avenue of that name, the Saint-Augustin church at the end of the Boulevard Malesherbes. A code established in the name of true beauty. Here again, let us denounce the deformation of accomplishments which had a harmonious origin: the Place de la Concorde is a notable composition: Gabriel's palaces, the rue Royale in the axis, and the Madeleine, one hundred and fifty meters away. Opposite, the Palais-Bourbon. A "classic" composition with a comprehensible axis; dimensions on a human scale. The spectacle is real, plastic. A royal composition. It is a place of glory, a porch of honor. It is not a street, much less a traffic artery. Let's not confuse things! Period of the carriage and pedestrian.

A city has a biological life. It is justly said of a man that he is "a digestive tube with an entrance and an exit." At the entrance or exit of the tube there is neither a church nor a palace. There is a free passage! A fundamental condition of health of a city is being traversed, irrigated, nourished from end to end, being free! Let's not graft plastic forms on this need which has a biological character. The occasion for that ought to be an appropriate one.

New York lives by its clear checkerboard. Millions of beings act simply and easily within it. Freedom of mind. From the first hour, the stranger is oriented, sure of his course.

We shall see that a plastic spectacle exists along the gigantic avenue. Also, that it could have a different character.

We shall see, further, that the street plan of Manhattan, proud and strong, established in colonial times, a model of wisdom and greatness of vision, is today in mortal danger because of the motorcar.

And that remedies as vigorous as the first plan are necessary, if the city does not wish to decline.

Life never stops. The torment of men will be eternal, unless the function of creating and acting and changing, living intensely through each day, be considered an eternal joy.

THE SKYSCRAPERS OF NEW YORK ARE TOO SMALL!

On the morning after my arrival in New York the *New York Herald Tribune* printed in big type, over my caricatured newspaper photograph:

FINDS AMERICAN SKYSCRAPERS MUCH TOO SMALL
Skyscrapers not big enough
Says Le Corbusier at first sight
Thinks they should be huge and a lot farther apart.

At two o'clock I disembarked from the ship; at four o'clock reporters had gathered at the Museum of Modern Art.

The cardinal question asked of every traveler on his arrival is: "What do you think of New York?" Coolly I replied: "The skyscrapers are too small."

And I explained what I meant.

For a moment my questioners were speechless! So much the worse for them! The reasoning is clear and the supporting proofs abundant, streets full of them, a complete urban disaster.

The skyscraper is not a plume rising from the face of the city. It has been made that, and wrongly. The plume was a poison to the city. The skyscraper is an instrument. A magnificent instrument for the concentration of population, for getting rid of land congestion, for classification, for internal efficiency. A prodigious means of improving the conditions of work, a creator of economies and, through that, a dispenser of wealth. But the skyscraper as plume, multiplied over the area of Manhattan, has disregarded experience. The New York skyscrapers are out of line with the rational skyscraper which I have called: *the Cartesian skyscraper* ("Plans," *Revue internationale*, Paris, 1931).[1]

Let me explain the Cartesian skyscraper:

a) First of all, *it is realizable*, thanks to modern techniques: bold steel skeletons; lifting machinery; technique of sound-proofing. Extraordinary perfection of electric lighting, creation of precisely *conditioned air*, demonstrated efficiency of elevators, etc. . . .

b) The skyscraper easily reaches a height of a thousand feet. Intuitively, I accept sixty stories, or seven hundred and twenty feet, a dimension that seems to me good.[2]

c) The skyscraper is normally vertical, plumb, from top to bottom, without setbacks or slopes—unlike the New York skyscrapers, handled nonsensically as the result of a deplorably romantic city ordinance.

d) The skyscraper is a light radiator, which means that no office surface can be deprived of solar light. Consequently, it should have a form independent of that belonging to the ground plot, and developing from its three fundamental organs: elevators, corridors, offices planned with a depth directly proportioned to the height of the windows.

e) The skyscraper should not have offices on the north side. Its layout will depend on the path of the sun in the sky—which should be diagrammed. Combined with the necessities of stability, of resistance to the wind (the greatest adversary of the skyscraper), it will take, in plan, a characteristic form.

1 Article in the "Ville Radieuse" series: "Is Descartes an American?"
2 "A Contemporary City for Three Million People." Autumn Salon. Paris, 1922.

f) The skyscraper is built of steel—a skeleton woven like a filigree in the sky, a spidery thing, marvelously clear and free. There are no *walls* in the skyscraper, since a wall is not easily put in place at six hundred and fifty feet; why have one anyway? Until the introduction of new methods of construction in reinforced concrete or steel, a wall served to *support* floors. Today they are carried by posts which do not take up a thousandth part of the surface of the ground, and not by walls. The exterior of the skyscraper, the façade—the façades—can be a film of glass, a skin of glass. Why repudiate richness itself: floods of light coming in.

g) The skyscraper should be large. It can contain ten thousand, twenty thousand, thirty thousand, forty thousand occupants easily. It is worthwhile, then, to arrange its approaches and flawless means of transportation: subways, buses or trolleys, roads for cars.

h) Now we are ready to state the fundamental principle: the skyscraper *is a function of capacity* (the offices) *and of the area of free ground at its base.* A skyscraper which does not fulfill this function harmoniously is a disease. That is the disease of New York.

The Cartesian skyscraper is a miracle in the urbanization of the cities of machine civilization. It makes possible extraordinary concentrations, from three to four thousand persons on each two and one-half acres. It does so while taking up only 8 to 12 per cent of the ground, 92 to 88 per cent being restored, usable, available for the circulation of pedestrians and cars! These immense free areas, this whole ward in the business section, will become a park. The glass skyscrapers will rise up like crystals, clean and transparent in the midst of the foliage of the trees. It is sufficient to discover the proper relation of parcels of ground, of skyscraper distribution, of their spacing, of their capacity. A new law appears among the rules of this new game: the technical conditions of automobile traffic. It requires a new dimensioning of the stages between the intersections of automobile highways; the right spacing of these highways.

This must be explained still further: if the skyscraper is large enough, the expenses of foundations are immediately divided up among admirably efficient installations: the common services of the skyscraper restaurants, bars, showrooms, barber shops, dry-goods stores, etc. . . . Office life, made intensely productive through mechanical rationalization: post office, telephone, telegraph, radio, pneumatic tubes, etc. . . . thus the benefit of excellent psycho-physiological conditions: luxury, perfection, quality in the whole building—halls, elevators, the offices themselves (quiet and pure air). Here I call to mind the business offices of Paris; ah! wretched, mediocre and miserable offices, an unsuspected degradation of the spirit of work—those entrances, those grotesque, ridiculous, idiotic elevators, those dark and bleak vestibules, and the series of dim rooms open on the hubbub of the street or on the dreariness of courts. Ah! no, let no one continue to defend the "good-natured" charm of these Homaisian installations where nothing, nothing, is efficient. I repeat: where the spirit is afflicted. Already in New York Rockefeller Center affirms to the world the dignity of the new times by its useful and noble halls, just as the skyscraper of Howe and Lescaze does in Philadelphia.

Here I wish to evoke the true splendor of the Cartesian skyscraper: the tonic spectacle, stimulating, cheering, radiant, which, from each office, appears through the transparent glass walls leading into space. Space! That response to the aspiration of the human being, that relaxation for breathing and for the beating heart, that outpouring of self in looking far, from a height, over a vast, infinite, unlimited expanse. Every bit of sun and fresh, pure air furnished mechanically. Do you try to maintain the fraud of hypocritical affirmations, to throw discredit on these radiant facts, to argue, to demand the "good old window," open on the stenches of the city and street, the noise, air currents, and the company of flies and mosquitoes? For thirty years I have known the offices of Paris: conversations cut to pieces by the uproar, suffocating atmosphere, the view broken thirty feet

away by the walls of houses, dark corners, half-light, etc. . . .
Impostors should no longer deny the gains of our period and by
their fright prevent changing from one thing to another, keeping
the city or cities in general from going their joyously destined
way.

The skyscrapers of New York are too small and there are too
many of them. They are proof of the new dimensions and the
new tools; the proof also that henceforth everything can be carried out on a new general plan, a symphonic plan—extent and
height.

Their history is mixed up with questions of utility and questions of vanity. They built tall buildings in Wall Street because
it was necessary to be grouped around the Stock Exchange, in
order to be able to act quickly. One sees canyons surging up,
deep and violent fissures, streets such as no one had ever seen
before. Not ugly either! I will even say: a very strong architectural sensation which is equal to that experienced in the narrow
streets of Rouen and Toulon, with in this case the enthronement
of a grandeur and intensity well calculated to inspire courage.
Later, I shall speak of one of the most remarkable architectural
sights in the world: the face of Washington seen against the
Doric columns of the Sub-Treasury, at the foot of the cliff
formed by the skyscrapers of Wall Street.

The skyscrapers born out of national conditions in Wall
Street multiplied thereafter, first on that site, establishing the
mystically alluring city seen far out at sea by the traveler, which
gives him a high idea of American destiny before suddenly as-
saulting him, a half hour later, with its savagery and brutality,
when the boat comes into direct contact with it in the Hudson.

The skyscrapers then disappear in an area of several miles,
an urban no man's land made up of miserable low buildings—
poor streets of dirty red brick. They spring up again suddenly in
mid-town (the center of the city) much higher, fitted out with
"architecture" and charged with a mission; the proclamation of

a proper name, that of a financial success, a fortune, a monetary power. Thus in the Middle Ages, at San Gimignano in Tuscany, the struggles for control among the families of the little city brought about the construction of fantastically high towers, one after another, each one higher than the last; height indicated the triumph of one family and the crushing of another. San Gimignano has the appearance of a pincushion, and the spectacle delights tourists while troubling common sense; hirsute beauty —yes, beauty, why not? The cataclysms of nature—jagged rocks, Niagara, Alps, or canyons, do they not compel our admiration by the effect of power, the feeling of catastrophe? In New York, it is by a thousand feet of height that the game is played—the game of skyscrapers, the sport of skyscrapers. Those mad Americans, how they have enjoyed themselves! Competition—football, boxing, the risky diversions of cowboys—there is a quality of spirit in all that. They celebrate the completion of each skyscraper. There are festivities, while building everyone laughs, is gay, fires rockets: a success is crowned. The troubadours of the new world sing of their loves. That was during the period of prosperity. Friends! it is all new, it is the burst of youth of a new world; there are in the world, in Manhattan, new white cathedrals.

They are sublime, naïve, touching, idiotic. I admire the enthusiasm which projects them into the sky. In the Olympic Games their pole vaulters surpass previous world records. Theirs are record skyscrapers.

From that task, once accomplished, resulted the death of the city at the base. The ground was killed. The fields should have been preserved. The overwhelmed local authorities inconsiderately allowed a policy of laissez faire. Nevertheless, they intervened in order to encourage further these floral games. The lawmakers concerned themselves with preventing a nocturnal darkness in the streets, in full daylight. Is their intention supported by rational considerations? No legislation has ever been so contrary to common sense. The laws forbid skyscrapers rising vertically from their bases; thus the skyscraper will become a pyramid, will fade away from the street, will slide into oblique wall surfaces and will appear to be a stylus flanked by other styluses. The drawings supplied in support of the law show that the Cartesian spirit was brushed aside in conceiving this ravishing delirium: they wanted to do something "beautiful," "living," "triumphant." They wished to make the city a tiara of innumerable cathedrals. In the twentieth century, a period of the steel skeleton and big money, everything was sacrificed to a thought which was in some ways disinterested. The debate was not dragged out, as with us, through fifty years of disputes between architects' councils, supported by magazines and exhibitions of projects on paper. No. It is in this that the USA is the USA. The city was constructed at a tremendous rate; it sprang up vertically, a skyscraper every month or it may be every three months. Skyscrapers? The city is full of them, the sky is full of them; from below it is a prodigious flaming holocaust. Let no one say lightly that Americans act only in order to pile up dollars. Here they have given proof of the strength of their enthusiasm, of their youthful openness, of their nascent exuberance.

During this epic period, in Paris—Paris stimulated by these new cries—the magistrates responsible for the destiny of the city were also trying to legislate: the six-story houses heretofore allowed are too high; their height should be limited by law to four stories. In particular, the thirty-three kilometers of the zone fortified by Napoleon III, in process of destruction, was involved; money questions cut short so many "high" thoughts. In ten years —while New York moved as a unit to a position of leadership through its gigantic undertakings—were constructed the thirty kilometers of low cost housing of the City of Paris which will remain in history. Will it be a glaring proof of definitive abdication? "French" was opposed to "American." Without ever going to see what was there, they definitively ennobled "French" by a flattering characterization: measure, our beautiful measure.

These flowers of perfumed rhetoric covered a little the disturbing musty odor which assailed our noses.

Everything finally bears fruit, a tangible result was attained: the socialist commune of Boulogne, independent of Paris though representing an eminent industrial and working-class district of Paris, animated by the purest intentions, saddled itself with a magistrate's law forbidding thenceforth buildings of more than four stories. At the edge of this commune, on the very border of the zone of Napoleon III, I succeeded in completing the last normal six-story building, and I personally live in the attic com-prising the seventh and eighth stories. I live at an altitude of seventy-two feet while my friend Harrison works at a height of eight hundred and twenty feet in Rockefeller Center. And when we take the elevator at the same moment, we arrive at our doors at the same time, in forty-five seconds. Reader, I ask you this: was not Delaisi, in naming one of his books *The Contradictions of the Modern World*, already aware that the world goes around badly and that in this century of certitudes we are submerged in incertitudes?

During these ten years New York raised itself into the sky; but the Soviets in Moscow denounced the skyscraper as "capi-talist." A denaturing of the objects in question.

During this time, also, New York, having built too many skyscrapers too small, ossified its soil, disorganized the streets to such an extent that the city officials are still disturbed by it. They no longer know what to do with their city, their streets, their destroyed circulation. In the beautiful maritime sky of Manhattan they have made sparkling cathedrals for themselves.

I am not dismayed. Americans are strong enough to admit that this tremendous flowering of the "boom period" should be demolished and replaced by structures which are noble, but also efficient. The skyscraper as a useful instrument, a function of height and the area of available ground, that is the next task for New York. It will be the third metamorphosis of the city. Later on in the book, I shall explain this matter technically.

THE SKYSCRAPERS ARE GREATER
THAN THE ARCHITECTS

I was in a mood for joking when I landed in America! That was my answer two days later, to a question from my friend Brooks, a *New York Times* editor. By that statement I meant to say that the notable thing about American skyscrapers today is their height. It is a question of footage, of quantity, with architecture, character, the architectural miracle, completely disregarded.

I was as it were shocked by the lack of architectural imagination in so many places where one is in a position to recognize the quality of a discovery. I shall speak later of the psychological significance of such failures. The USA is a country of boldness or courage and of great uneasiness, two states which are connected, moreover, and which are productive when they are in the right proportions.

It is an odd thing that the modern skyscrapers are the weak ones. The Italian Renaissance skyscrapers are of excellent quality, in contradiction with what I imagined before seeing them. For, prior to 1925, Brunelleschi and Palladio were in control. After 1925, after the plaster fanfares of our historic Exhibition of Decorative Arts—an event which made it possible for the masses to express a desire for "modern living" and which revealed that the professional world was not at all prepared to respond to that excellent aspiration; the result was the fixing of an indigent "1925 style," flat and false, made of plaster, for barbershops—the Americans made the plunge. By their works they prove to us what a long and deep effort is required to bring into being a genuine architecture. They did not measure up to their task; this modern architecture is poverty-stricken as much in its ensemble as in its detail; for that reason I consider it ephemeral; its years are numbered. Nevertheless, since they are building over there, they accomplish something, they increase their experience, already progress is appearing, evolution is in process. An impeccable quality of execution quite properly compels our admiration. Academicians of France, drowsing in official armchairs, know that New York builds infinitely better than we do, incomparably better, and that American workmen are the masters of the building trades—a title of honor transmitted through the centuries which a general decay has injured in our country. The locksmiths and masons of America are our masters.

In New York, then, I learn to appreciate the Italian Renaissance. It is so well done that you could believe it to be genuine. It even has a strange, new firmness which is not Italian but American! The maritime atmosphere and the potential of the American adventure have lifted the Tuscan graces to a new tone. The oldest skyscrapers of Wall Street add the superimposed orders of Bramante all the way up to the top with a clearness in molding and proportion which delights me. Here is an achieved perfection, repeated elsewhere in certain hotels, in numerous vast apartment houses on Park Avenue, a perfection strictly American. The contrary is found in the Customs House, near Wall Street, done in pure "Beaux-Arts" (as the Americans say; read: Ecole des Beaux-Arts de Paris) which, directly inspired by the Orsay Station or the Grand Palais in Paris, strikes a disagreeable note. So much insipidity and pomposity cannot resist the tonic air of the estuary.

I have dinner with Louis Carré in the dining room of the Gotham, done in a markedly Italian Renaissance style: coffered ceiling, wainscot in dark wood. On the white linen, exuberant, "over-rich" silver. It all has a strong unity. The American aspires to luxury, to ease, and to their sonorous forms of richness. A poor little modern style glass ash tray, bordered with red stripes "à la Marinot," accidentally placed among the heavy silver and sparkling glassware on our table, is quite disagreeable to look at.

American architects are tending to break away from the instruction of the Ecole des Beaux-Arts de Paris. A style is being born among them. Already the skyscrapers are standing. For the moment the skyscrapers are greater than the architects.

IN THE CELLARS!

For two and a half months I did not see a stairway in America! They are something that has been buried. They exist nevertheless, off each corridor, but hidden behind a door that you are not supposed to open. There is a lighted sign above the door: *Exit*. The stair can be used in case of panic or fire. But there are no fires in skyscrapers. Already they are large enough to have their own public services, including firemen. And there are fire extinguishers, hydrants, all the necessary preventive devices. How beautiful, clean, gleaming, this apparatus is, and always kept in good order and ready to use! There is, besides, the control center: the eye that sees everything, the brain that perceives everything, "the nerve center" as they call it. It is a glass cage with a man in it who has a large black panel in front of him which is covered with bulbs. From time to time this one or that one lights up in red or green or yellow. They explained the mechanism to me; I have forgotten it. Essentially, it is this: everywhere in the skyscrapers there are thin "guardian" tubes equipped with temperature recording instruments. When the temperature rises several degrees above normal, a bulb lights up on the panel. A bell rings. The place is known immediately. The telephone comes into play; a warning is given. Workmen go to that spot through hidden service passages planned for that purpose. The glass cage is diabolical.

Consider the most recent skyscraper, Rockefeller Center. It is rational, logically conceived, biologically normal, harmonious in its four functional elements: halls for the entrance and division of crowds, grouped shafts for vertical circulation (elevators), corridors (internal streets), regular offices.

Already the skyscraper is large enough to have made it possible to spend the money necessary to do a good job. The sets of bronze and glass doors are constructed with a machine-like rigor. In passing, I should mention that other skyscraper in Wall Street which is assailed by an endles crowd, a procession of visitors in a constant ebb and flow. You enter: when you are three feet away from the entrance you have chosen, the door opens of its own accord. You are going out; the door opens again. What is the *intelligence* breathed into so many doors across the entrance? They explain: notice the glass bulb which appears in front of each door, on the level of your hips; an invisible infra-red ray radiates from it horizontally; when you step within three feet of the door, your body intercepts the invisible ray; an electric circuit is established which operates an opening mechanism. It will open thus, automatically, ten thousand times a day if necessary.

Now we are in the hall of Rockefeller Center. There are sixty-five stories above it. The groups of elevators are divided into four categories: first, local, from the ground floor to the fifteenth floor; second, express, from the first floor to the sixteenth floor, and from there local to the thirtieth floor; third . . . likewise. Finally, express elevators to the sixty-fifth floor where there are living rooms, a restaurant, a large club, a terrace. Speed: thirteen hundred feet per minute. (In France, one hundred ninety-five feet.) In forty-five seconds you are at the top. Your ears feel it a little at first, but not your heart, so perfect are these machines. There are four or five groups with eight or twelve elevators in each. One elevator can accommodate twenty persons. The working of the doors is extremely ingenious, supple, and safe. There is an operator for each elevator. France alone has a monopoly on the fatal notice printed on a placard set askew on the wall:

The elevator is out of order. My American auditors roared with laughter when I told them that the obstacle always raised by European opponents against my suggestions for a "radiant city" was this: "Elevators don't work!" or: "But suppose the elevator doesn't work!" In America the elevators do work, just as the water in the pipes, the lighting of the streets work, as do the trains in the stations, etc. . . . . It is something that has been accomplished; there is no longer any discussion about it. It may be said that in New York the construction of elevators has reached a moving technical and plastic perfection. A conquest of modern times, a product of selection, of worthy architecture; a feast for the eyes and the spirit.[1]

This quality of workmanship I noted again in the Philadelphia skyscraper already mentioned, which houses a bank, where it is present to an astonishing degree. It is coquetry, coquetry in choice steels; the ventilators, the doors of safes are so extremely well made that I wrote in my notebook: "They are gods." Yes, a

---

1 I had just written these lines about the accomplished certitudes of vertical circulation. The next day (exactly) the Paris paper carried the headline: "The elevator operators of New York are on strike!" Well then, life in Manhattan has stopped! It is a blow. My friends say: "Have you read about the strike?" I have thought about the question and I am not disturbed. We must not confuse things. I have shown that the architectural revolution was brought about as the result of modern techniques. That is my province. Certitudes allow me to carry on my researches.

The elevator operators are on strike? That is a question of social revolution. Strikes are effective instruments for demanding rights. The elevator operators are not making a living? What can machinery do about that! The business activity of New York is at a standstill? That is a fact; it is a proof of failure in social and economic organization.

In fact I am glad that it happened. Be reassured: Americans will not stop building and using skyscrapers. They will try to bring the social and economic machine into equilibrium.

I will go further: it is fortunate that such "incidents" occur. Our cities, our "radiant cities" cannot be built on the basis of our present legislation. The sap of the new times must circulate in worn-out, cruel, inhuman organizations. The new times are near! We shall be able to estimate them through the revolutions which still must take place.

perfection which reaches the highest nobility. I added: "May the French send their craftsmen to visit American engineers."

The secret of such a success lies in the flawless and rigorous division of responsibilities among technicians grouped in a *team* for the study and carrying out of these vast American constructions. Here there is not *one* architect, but several, chosen for their particular qualifications: one who knows how to organize circulation; one who is familiar with the problems of offices; one who can "compose" a plan; one who can design a façade; one for the necessary calculations; finally, the head architect who is the general organizer and supervisor. Then comes the legion of special engineers for air conditioning, telephones, windows, electricity, elevators, the legal counsel, etc. . . . They work as a group, that is as a complete team from the start. Everything is planned synchronously and synthetically at the beginning of the job. Such constructions have a perfect and faultless life.

For instance, when I visited the immense vertical dock of the Port of New York, I noticed freight elevators twenty feet wide and forty-five feet deep directly entered by loaded trucks (up to twenty-eight tons). They rise at the rate of two hundred feet per minute. Two double elevators serve fourteen stories—with landings for twelve trucks. At a proper distance the system is repeated. It adds up to nearly three hundred and thirty-six trucks being taken care of, loading and unloading it should be remembered without manual assistance. How many thousand trucks per day? More than that, the streets around the vertical dock are unencumbered.

I emphasize the question of the elevators because I consider it the key to all the urban reforms which will save our contemporary cities from disaster. We are far from being in general agreement: in our International Congresses on modern architecture—which were the advance guard—I met a stubborn resistance to solutions based on that modern tool; the resistance came from our Continental associates. In this connection also it is worthwhile to make a trip to America in order to realize *that a page has turned*.

In Europe we think and act too much without experimentation, so that our ideas of height, among others, are purely imaginary. In my *Radiant City* studies, I patiently sought for a building height which should remain *human*. I did not wish to lose myself in theory, in the stratosphere, and put people in conditions which would affront feeling, and more than that, psychophysiological reflexes. I accepted as reasonable a building height of one hundred and sixty feet. In New York my hotel room is on the twenty-first floor, about two hundred and twenty-five feet above the ground. I was greatly surprised to find that I had by no means lost contact with the ground. My myopic eyes easily, even very clearly, grasp the activities in the street—people, cars in movement. In offices on the sixty-fifth floor (about five hundred and eighty-five feet), this feeling of security persists. There is joined to it a joyous and exalting sensation of space, extent, freedom, which I had always imagined, and which I enjoy here to the fullest degree. There is no feeling of dizziness. We lose ourselves in academic discussions without any basis. Personal experience is the real test. Moreover, men have always tried to lift themselves up, to climb as high as possible.

Experimentation also instructs us about the other questions. For instance, my great colleague Auguste Perret, in an article about architecture in the *Nouvelle Encyclopédie française*, notes that street noises do not reach the fourteenth floor. He had already expressed the idea to me in a different way and I believe that I put it down in good faith in one of my books. Now, in New York, from the twenty-first floor, I hear all the noises, precisely and in detail, amplified even! I am stupefied. I cannot sleep with the window barely half open. Gustave Lyon would have explained it to us clearly: street noises will reach the thousandth floor if conditions are right for it. That is, if around my skyscraper there are building walls disposed so as to serve as ricochet surfaces for street noise, projecting it a long distance by reflection—in this case vertically—and transmitting it exactly. The height has nothing to do with the case. Everything depends on the closeness of surrounding walls which may be disposed accidentally in such a way as to form a magnificent sound-projecting screen. Conclusion: One can rigorously control the placement of skyscrapers in such a way that no reflective surfaces are offered to street noises, and thus the desired silence can be secured.

Some other unexpected observations may be noted: certain strong winds cause the rain to sweep up the side of a skyscraper from bottom to top instead of from the top down. Windows designed for the natural fall of rain were found to be insufficient. It was necessary to modify them.

During a heavy storm, the Philadelphia skyscraper already mentioned undergoes such flexion that the office doors are temporarily jammed and cannot be opened. Unexpected problems encountered by people who are not fossilized. What a relief after the summer houses of the Paris suburbs!

And here is something that takes us back to them:

The skyscrapers of New York and Chicago are made of stone and not of glass. Whole quarries have been fastened to their steel skeletons by means of cramps, quarries suspended in empty space. It is inconceivable. I thought that I would find an erect city of steel. Not at all! It is a city of stone. I grant that the stone is beautiful under the maritime sky of New York. The sunsets are moving. The sunrises (I saw them) are admirable: in a violet fog or dull atmosphere the solar fanfare bursts forth like a salvo, raw and clean, on the surface of one tower, then another, then many others. An Alpine spectacle which lights up the vast horizon of the city. Rose crystals, rose stone. There are tiaras over it, sometimes gold-colored, and not at all comic in effect but often beautiful: the crown of the Tour de Beurre in Rouen and variations on it. The skyscraper as "plume" is not rational; it is quite natural however that the plume should be charming or luxurious.

But so much stone has everywhere left innnumerable small

windows, an infinity of windows, in Manhattan; they are all alike. Americans have established a type of window and they use it remorselessly throughout the USA. I should like to bring remorse to the souls of the architects and say to them: "In your offices, however high they may be, these cottage windows are annoying. They lead you up a blind alley: the space that you have gained by height—a treasure—is not being used, you do not seize it. You have missed out! In your eyries you seem to be in cellars!"

SOMETHING WHICH HAS BEEN ACCOMPLISHED

If your eyes could penetrate the opaque masses of the façades, they would see an incredible spectacle: three hundred thousand, five hundred thousand men and women—perhaps more—at work in a pool of space at the same time. A humanity having broken its millenary destiny which was to be attached to the ground, which is suspended between heaven and earth, going up and down at high speed in clusters of twenty and in sheaves of two hundred. Is it a new scene in purgatory?

It is modern society experimenting on a grand scale with the machinery which will someday enable it to create the "radiant city," when everything will be well calculated, justly valued, exactly measured out. An enormous amount of time will be saved every day. Make an effort to picture the "business activity" in Paris or elsewhere: hurried pedestrians, taxis immobilized at every corner, buses full of people anxious to go somewhere quickly, subways. Business activities are so dispersed and scattered about the city that many people lose a large share of their time in a sterile struggle with distance. Every day! What loss of energy, what waste!

Well, these innumerable pools of space in New York assure us that distance will be conquered when we have learned to make the right adjustments.

In place of so many small, scattered skyscrapers, a few large ones will be set up between 42nd Street and 55th Street, in groups. Distance will be overcome. And hours will be saved and usable.

In Algiers, a single skyscraper will suffice.

In Barcelona, two skyscrapers.

In Antwerp, three skyscrapers.

In its usable center, on condemned areas, Paris can raise an efficient and magnificent business community.

This much will have been accomplished: no longer will it be necessary for people to jostle each other on foot or in chained vehicles in a labyrinth of streets during rush hours. Business communities will be vertical, set in the midst of immense green parks.

When the cathedrals were white, no one thought that height was the sign of a degeneration of spirit.

A MILLION AND A HALF CARS DAILY

"The street plan of Manhattan, proud and strong, established in colonial times, a model of wisdom and greatness of vision, is today in mortal danger because of the motorcar."

I promised to return to that question.

The clear plan—like the similar ones of Buenos Aires and Barcelona—or the tangled plans of Paris or London, go back alike to the time of horses and oxcarts. Movement was at the rate of six kilometers per hour. Intersections normally came every fifty or one hundred and ten meters.

The day before my return to France I have lunch with the assistant police commissioner of New York. He wishes to impress me: "How many cars do you think there are in daily circulation in New York?" he asks me. I don't want to underestimate egregiously. Instead of saying fifty thousand, I reply: "Two million." "That's astonishing, you are quite close: there are a million and a half."

That is a detail which does not require comment.

Terrible automatic red and green traffic lights, which bring ten thousand yards of street traffic to a stop at one time and allow more than a hundred cross streets to function, extend their dictatorship over the whole metropolitan area and are an affliction to one's nerves. I was irritated, depressed, made ill by them. There can be no salvation—no more for New York than for Paris—if measures are not taken soon which take into consideration the scale established by the automobile.

November seventh there was a heavy rain; the streets became slippery; traffic was completely tied up. The next day the newspapers commented about it. It is an endemic condition apparently. An immediate solution is needed. The suggestion was made that the manufacture of motorcars be stopped for a year (Ford puts six thousand cars into circulation *every day!*). The production of cars is the largest industry in the USA. And then a hysterical solution is suggested! At regular intervals during the past ten years it has been proposed that pedestrians be taken care of by means of bridges, and that idea is repeated once more.

Naïveté and light-mindedness. The poor unnumbered and docile pedestrians are not the crux of the matter, they are only an accessory encumbrance: when the lights turn red they slip across in the path opened for the crossing cars. The question is not, *absolutely not at all*, that of pedestrians; the question is the intersection of cars at such short intervals. When the lights turn green, the cross traffic moves and the red light stops the other cars. The pedestrians take advantage of the stoppage to get across. The endless cutting of the avenues by the streets is the cause of the trouble, as the cause of the trouble in Paris is the endless cutting at short intervals of a complex and dense web of streets.

The automobile, traveling sixty miles an hour, cannot live in a street pattern of that kind. It needs a different sort of plan. Everywhere the great problem of modern times is the reconstitution of the street pattern for automobiles in a vastly larger network. I have proposed a network composed of units a quarter of a mile in length on each side. Then intersections will be far enough apart to make possible the ramps necessary for differences of level; no longer will there be stops at intersections; cars will move on one-way lanes, without stops.

The day after the storm in New York taxi drivers complained that they were no longer able to make a living. That evening it had taken them an hour or even more to get passengers to their destinations.

Finally, imagine the disaster caused by the overnumerous small skyscrapers. The blocks between streets and avenues, that is the building sites, are tiny parcels of land. In accordance with universal practice skyscrapers, like other buildings, are placed on the edge of the sidewalk, and shoot up straight from the street. To say skyscrapers is to say offices, that is, businessmen and automobiles. Can hundreds of cars park at the foot of skyscrapers? The necessary space is lacking, there as elsewhere. We in Paris are familiar with that problem in the business section around the Opera and the Champs Elysées. It is the end of everything. It is intolerable. The city officials say: "Nothing can be done about it." Paris is ill, but New York has hardening of the arteries. A skyscraper should not be a coquettish plume rising straight up from the street. It is a wonderful instrument of concentration, to be placed in the midst of vast open spaces. The density in the sky-scraper and the free area at the foot of the skyscraper constitute an indissoluble function. The one without the other is a catas-trophe. That is what New York has arrived at!

THERE ARE NO TREES IN THE CITY

There are no trees in the city! That is the way it is.

Trees are the friends of man, symbols of every organic cre-ation; a tree is an image of a complete construction. A delightful spectacle which appears to us in the most fantastic, yet perfectly ordered arabesques; a mathematically measured play of branches multiplied each spring by a new life-giving hand. Leaves with finely placed nerves. A cover over us between earth and sky. A friendly screen close to our eyes. A pleasant measure interposed between our hearts and eyes and the eventual geometries of our hard constructions. A precious instrument in the hands of the city planner. The most concentrated expression of the forces of nature. The presence of nature in the city, surrounding our la-bors or our pleasures. Trees are the millenary companions of man!

Sun, space, and trees are the fundamental materials of city planning, the bearers of the "essential joys." Considering them thus, I wished to restore urban man to the very heart of his natural setting, to his fundamental emotions. Deprived of trees, he exists with only the artificial frame of his own creations; it is proper that sometimes, on certain solemn occasions, he should affirm in all their rigor the purity and strength of his geometries. But deprived of trees in part or in the whole extent of cities in innumerable cases where nothing is planned, where everything is disagreeable and brutal, it is sad to be thus naked and impoverished, lost in the insecurity of a faltering order, in the arbitrariness of a fatal disorder.

Nevertheless, Central Park has been saved, in the middle of Manhattan.

You like to accuse Americans of being concerned only with making money? I am struck with admiration for the strength of character of the municipal authorities of New York who have preserved granite rocks and trees in the center of Manhattan, a park more than four and a half million square yards in area.

The park is surrounded by fine buildings—apartment houses in tall blocks or in the form of skyscrapers—all with windows opening on this unexpected space, a fairylike situation unique in the city without trees. If the precious ground of Central Park is valued at from two thousand to four thousand dollars per square yard, the commercial value of these granite rocks amounts to anywhere from ten billion to eighteen billion dollars. To keep this immense treasure untouchable in the very center of Manhattan, I think that that shows a high civic attitude, an extraordinary attitude. It is the sign of a strong society.

Paris measured out and sold the greatest part of its reserve of air and space in the Champ-de-Mars, about 1910, after having committed a prior sacrilege: the destruction of the Hall of Machines, an iron cathedral.

A REMARKABLE ARCHITECTURAL SIGHT

(From a short talk in response to the speech of welcome by Mr. Philip Goodwin, chairman of the architectural section of the Museum of Modern Art, on the occasion of a lunch for members of various architectural associations in New York, held on the sixty-fifth floor of Radio City.)

"In the intense heart of Wall Street, city of banks, at the exciting end of one of the canyons formed by skyscrapers, I experienced the shock of a remarkable architectural spectacle. There, I think, is the strongest and noblest plastic composition (for the moment) in the USA. The bronze statue of Washington stands on the steps of the Sub-Treasury in front of the Doric porch; above are the rough-hewn early skyscrapers, rising vertically and making it a compact lap dominated by a gigantic chest of geometrically organized stones pierced by innumerable window squares, against an endless extent of tangled surfaces of vertical shafts; the materials are varied, the crowning elements against the sky are in confusion. On the right angle formed by the arch of the eyebrow and the nose, where the eye is placed, the mask of Washington focuses the whole mass of this immense landscape of stone. There he is, quite near, raised several feet above the pavement; the steps of the Sub-Treasury, fearfully steep, have a sharp and threatening quality. The clean, ordered range of Doric columns takes hold of the limited open space and projects it into the air toward the skyscrapers which are like a splendid natural phenomenon, one of those places where nature or the imagination of men has delighted to place the seat of the gods.

"There is disparity: John Ward's Washington; the Doric order of the Theseum in Athens; the walls of American business. . . . I assure you that this is a mathematically organized space, that a perfect mathematical harmony exists in it, through the occurrence of a happy accident.

"Likewise, on the Acropolis of Athens, spaces and volumes disposed by topography and by perfect knowledge, associated with a circle of mountains and facing the island-dotted sea, have made this site dear to our hearts.

"For those who are able to see, New York, projected violently into the sky, an outcry that you hate and love at the same time, hides in the bottom of its canyons of banks the architectural composition which is most expressive of the soul of the country. An architectural scene variously put together, majestic, intense, remarkable. The foursquare mask of Washington is at the exact point from which the tumultuous forces of architecture are set in play. Proportion, quantities, relations, absolute mathematical rightness, radiance . . ."

A PLACE OF RADIANT GRACE

At the opposite end of the city—Wall Street being at the south end of Manhattan—at the northern extremity of the island, the George Washington Bridge spans the Hudson—an arm of the sea or an estuary rather than a river. The floor of the bridge, as in other bridges, is high enough to allow the passage of large ships. Thus the approaches have to be carefully designed ramps which gradually dominate the city. American bridges are of the suspension type. That expresses a trait of mind. What are bridges for? To enable you to cross over on a horizontal platform, but also to allow a free space below for the passage of boats: that principle is accepted everywhere. Monumental arches? They are not in question, it is a question of a bridge! Daring is a virtue, and, assisted by technique, it has made possible at certain happy moments the attainment of architectural splendor.

The George Washington Bridge over the Hudson is the most beautiful bridge in the world. Made of cables and steel beams, it gleams in the sky like a reversed arch. It is blessed. It is the only seat of grace in the disordered city. It is painted an aluminum color and, between water and sky, you see nothing but the bent cord supported by two steel towers. When your car moves up the ramp the two towers rise so high that it brings you happiness; their structure is so pure, so resolute, so regular that here, finally, steel architecture seems to laugh. The car reaches an unexpectedly wide apron; the second tower is very far away; innumerable vertical cables, gleaming against the sky, are suspended from the magisterial curve which swings down and then up. The rose-colored towers of New York appear, a vision whose harshness is mitigated by distance.

The bridge has a story which almost turned out ridiculously. Mr. Cullman, president of the Port of New York, told me about it. The bridge was constructed under his supervision. The problem required the utmost engineering boldness. Calculation aided by a fortunate hypothesis gave the work the severity of things which are exact. The bridge leaps over the Hudson in a single bound. Two steel-topped concrete piers between the banks and the apron hold the suspension chains. I have mentioned the extraordinary dimensions of the two towers. Constructed of riveted steel they stand up in the sky with a striking nobility. Now the towers were to have been faced with stone molded and sculptured in "Beaux-Arts" style (New York term for the aesthetic ideas current on the quai Voltaire in Paris).

Someone acted before it was too late. Then the whole committee of the Port of New York Authority. Little by little the spirit of modern times makes itself felt: these men said, "Stop! no stone or decoration here. The two towers and the mathematical play of the cables make a splendid unity. It is one. That

is the new beauty." They made some calculations; the maintenance of the towers by proper painting would cost an amount
equal to the interest on the capital which would have been in-
vested in stone-faced towers. Thus the two proposals were finan-
cially equivalent. They were not looking for a means of saving
expense. But "in the name of beauty and of the spirit" they
dismissed the architect with his decorations. Those men are
citizens!

Throughout this account I have been speaking of things
done on a grand scale. Through personal experience I know
that it is necessary to have seen; I do not care for literary evocations. Drawing cannot give you the inexpressible sensation of a
work thus suspended between water and sky. Neither can pho-
tography. The reader of these lines, then, will not be able to
appreciate as I do, in the fervor of his heart, the miracle which
happened at the right moment, when a sensitive and sober-
minded man cried: "Stop!"

In my lecture at Columbia University I began with the
evocation of the bridge and thanked the unknown man who had
saved it and had given to New York that place of grace and joy.

BROOKLYN BRIDGE

One fresh November morning—Indian summer prolongs
the fine, sunny days up to the threshold of the new year—I had
myself driven to the far end of the Brooklyn Bridge, on the left
bank of the East River, and I returned to Manhattan on foot,

over the bridge. It is a long distance on the foot walk and you are surrounded or dominated by the lanes for elevateds and cars. The sky before you bristles with the skyscrapers of Wall Street; they are rose-colored, gay, in the maritime sky. They are shaggy, crowned with gold or debatable architectural ornament. A violent feeling takes hold of you: the feeling of unanimity. There should be sensations of contriteness, of troubled judgment and taste, reservations, doubt, cacophony. But no! There is a dominating force: unity; a subjugating element: magnitude.

Yes! let us recognize that America has given us that sensation: magnitude which is noble, which can be very noble, as it often was in the past. Imagine the white cathedrals in an incompletely finished world, erect, straight, above the small houses. We have no right to inveigh against magnitude. Nor do we have the right to fall back on an egoism based on laziness and invoke "measure." We did not come to the USA to look for measure, but to look for conviction and enthusiasm.

Our European wearinesses require a tonic. I can hear the traitors, the defeatists, the sanctimonious people in France; later on I shall speak of a French professor who came to New York University to fulfill a sacred mission(!). "I try to teach them good taste and measure." You do not walk into a battlefield or into one of the vast workshops of the world in dress clothes and patent leather shoes, mouthing discourses. Too many complacent people do nothing but carp and talk like Pompadours to sweating nations caught in the tentacles of the struggle for life.

Brooklyn Bridge, which is old (elevateds, cars, trucks, pedestrians all have special lanes), is as strong and rugged as a gladiator, while George Washington Bridge, built yesterday, smiles like a young athlete. In this case the two large Gothic towers of stone are very handsome because they are American and not "Beaux-Arts." They are full of native sap and they are not graceful, but strong. The vertical cables are black and not silver, but in perspective their vertical fall fixes a spidery veil. It is an imposing architectural sensation; vertical, slender, immense, yes, I come

back to *the immense* and like a barbarian I enjoy it, or better, as
a man animated by a constructive spirit, active but wearied by
the depressing atmosphere of cowardice and abdication in Paris,
crushed, often dishonored, treated as a madman and Utopian,
consigned to the Greek calends, etc. . . . here I find *reality*. And
it brings me a profound satisfaction.

Reality, that is the lesson of America. It gives our boldest
speculation the certainty of imminent birth.

GRAND CENTRAL TERMINAL

The station, which is the terminus of railways running north
and west and serving innumerable suburbs, does not attract
attention to itself in the midst of Manhattan by means of domes
and pediments. It is an interior on the ground level, with base-
ments, where complete trains arrive from distant points, but
underground, under the houses, skyscrapers, and pavements of
New York.

To speak of American trains is to speak of something quite
different from the dull gloom of our conveyances. Grand Central Terminal is a marvel, and I am not referring to the technical
accomplishment of the engineers. I am speaking simply as an
ordinary traveler and I say that taking a train here is a pleasure
excursion.

First, it is clean. It is kept clean constantly by an army of
excellent Negroes who are polite, attentive, and never obnoxi-
ously grasping. Back in France, I am pleased to observe that the

porters of the Paris stations, organized in a Baggage Transfer Union, give us, after so many discouraging years, the spectacle of a well-managed, productive, and healthy modern social cell: impeccable cleanliness, obligingness, courtesy, and amiability. They pool what they make and they have succeeded, after all hope had been given up, in getting rid of disorder. The porters in the Paris stations are as good as the Negroes in Grand Central Terminal or the Pennsylvania Station. That is a compliment; I will even say that they are much better and that can give us courage; other enterprises in the country will do as well some day, re-establishing the fundamental function of production.

In Grand Central cars come up carefully planned ramps to the ground level for departures; they go down to the basement for arrivals. Below, a hall of modest size with the Information Desk in the center; it has an architectural character; the personnel answer your questions as quickly as a barman would serve you elsewhere. If you ask when trains leave, you are given a printed timetable. There are many ticket windows all around you. Between the large corridors leading to the subways and the ramps going up and down there are public services: shops with useful articles, restaurants, etc. . . .

Where are the trains? From time to time a modest iron gate opens. In front of it there are ticket-checking booths and neatly uniformed employees. You pass through and descend a ramp. The platform stretches away with trains on either side; the floor of the coaches is on a level with the platform. Yes! As it is also in England. I have never been able to understand why, in our country and in so many others, people are asked to walk up and down the narrow, hazardous steps of coaches.

The crowds come and go, quickly absorbed by the gates leading to the platforms. The beautiful stone slabs of the floor are shining and spotless at all times. Papers never lie about on it. And, coming from a distant place or from the suburbs, you arrive in the heart of New York. Or you leave for some distant point in trains which are also very different from ours.

SUBURBAN TRAINS

Nevertheless, in a surreptitious way, the tumor of the *great American waste* fastens itself upon this magic station. Grand Central is the head of the gigantic suburbs of Connecticut. Luxurious trains, agreeable servants of exodus. Leave! It is the proof of an urban existence which has been upset, turned upside down. In the course of my talks in the USA, my thought concerned itself more and more with this great evil of the USA: the excessive extension of urban regions, the prodigious—and mad— networks of railways, of roads; a whole people in eternal and sterile movement; the hurry, the agitation, failure of action. Hundreds of thousands of houses pushing nature into the distance and spoiling it; conduits for water, gas, electricity, telephone, which go to each house! A gigantic expense, an immense burden on the nation, a bewildering social deficit . . .

The suburban trains are so handsome that they nourish ruinous illusions. I am speaking of the suburban trains which serve people in comfortable circumstances and not of the purgatory which extends from the subways to the varied hells of the slums. They furrow immense distances; they get mixed up with the main lines running into New England, prolonging the New York region indefinitely and endowing the New Yorker with a special biology! He is a being fitted out with wheels; he drives constantly, from the skyscraper elevators to his colonial style cottage, in the midst of forests, along the indented seacoast, or across prairies and through orchards. One thing leading to another (and you hardly know which of the two factors is leading the dance), he has developed the automobile in an astonishing way or, having the automobile at his disposal, he has enormously extended the radius of daily rounds. He closes the cycle by complementary installations: a miraculous telephone—which works as surely as the elevators do—an instantaneous telephone; then, to fill up all the vacant time spent sitting in a Pullman or coach, he has made the newspaper into something monumental. He has created—along with certain well-done, serious sections: domestic and foreign politics—sections about domestic life, sport, radio, movies, to such an extent that the paper is quite heavy. Further, he is pleased by advertising which offers him the limitless seductions of everything that can be used or bought for the sake of becoming useful, practical, efficient, etc. . . . Also, he has created reviews, newsstand magazines, some of which are astonishingly luxurious (how is it possible?). Finally, they still read books. A large part of a New Yorker's life is spent in reading to pass away the time. That is good for business: paper business, printing, advertising. Advertising! With a fisherman's attention (in this case he accepts the role of a gudgeon) he watches for the advertising device which will tempt him, which will cause him to risk some little adventure, which will be entertaining, or have a clever turn. Time passes. How much time? Three hours a day do not frighten him. The train stops. His car is there at the station, left locked at eight o'clock in the morning and waiting for him at eight o'clock in the evening. The car is a useful tool and not an external indication of wealth. Perfect mass-produced tools, easy to handle, economical and not really expensive to buy. You return to your family where your wife, left early in the morning, is waiting for you. Later on, I shall attempt some unexpected observations about this suburban phenomenon.

On my return from Yale, in a Pullman car which is quite comfortable because of its freedom from the crowding of the coaches, in which you can move about, or turn in any direction on a rotating chair, which has the tranquil, easygoing atmosphere of a club room, I talk to a professor from the University who explains to me what he has finally consented to accept every day in his life. "I leave my house early, I park the car at the station, get on the train, change trains, arrive at Yale. And I do the same thing in the evening, in the other direction. I read, you see how comfortable it is. It is clear that we have created all kinds of comforts. Obviously we use them, we all use them and perhaps we do not have the time to digest anything: we do not have a minute in our lives in which we can make *appraisals* and nothing leads us to make *appraisals*, that is, to try to go to the bottom of things. We are in a whirlwind, we are the whirlwind, we do not have good judgment about anything that is outside of the whirlwind."

One Monday morning, I took one of the immense trains which drain Connecticut and pour out on the ramps of Grand Central the crowds of people necessary for the life of the city. There are no interior partitions in the coaches; they are large units of space with closed windows. Air conditioning supplies constantly renewed pure air. One of the cars of the train is a bar and grillroom; there are small tables to the right and left of the grill; on the long free side there is a counter with rotating stools. You have breakfast there: milk, hot chocolate, eggs, bacon, etc. . . . You serve yourself.

Throughout the train there is a characteristic cleanliness. There is only one smoking car. It is rather skimpy! Young women come in to smoke Chesterfields or Camels (fifteen cents a pack). (The French administration sells them to us in Paris for sixty-six cents! Likewise, another office has tripled the price of Ford cars in France.) The American countryside is rural; a large part of the horror of suburbs is eliminated in America because *there are no walls* around houses and estates. Nowhere. The houses spring up in prairies, surrounded by trees. That gives the landscape a kind of amplitude which is new to us. I like the walls of our old villages; they were modest, fitting, and always handled in an architectural way. I mean that those smooth and dignified walls disregarded the three *orders of architecture* and the lucubrations of architectural draughtsmen. But our suburbs are modern, the fruit of the instruction of the schools and of the taste for an appearance of "richness"; they are discouraging.

We have finally reached the outskirts of New York which

are as frightful as the center of Paris or Berlin. The train plunges
into a tunnel, passes under the river and stops in Grand Central.

THE FAIRY CATASTROPHE

New York is an event of worldwide importance. I have
called it the first place in the world on the scale of the new
times, the work yard of our era. Twenty years ago New York was
still only a strange, faraway city; we had a somewhat harsh opinion of the people and their city; we said: "America, 'way off
there." And we remained quiet in our acts and thoughts, bound
to the old scale. But the world broke out here and there; it was
swollen with sap and swollen with pus; the eruption floods the
world with pus and sap. New York, strong, proud of itself, in
prosperity or in depression, is like an open hand above our heads.
An open hand which tries to knead the substance of today. New
York has a style, has style, is mature enough to have acquired
style. There are not just ragged things there; there is quality. A
spirit is asserting itself; it shows itself in a section of Fifth Avenue, beside Central Park, or along Park Avenue; the people, the
shops, the products, the architecture, have achieved a character
which is grand, intense, and healthy. It is full of life; they are
places of robust life. The Place de l'Opéra in Paris is no longer
anything but a relic.
    Americans tell you: "New York is not America." They are
very conscious of it, they recognize themselves more readily in
New England, in Boston, city of thought and meditation; in

Chicago, rival of New York; in the innumerable "American" cities (ah! yes, what a unitary character in the gridiron plans, the extraordinary vigor, the activity); and then there is the diversity of this immense territory in which France, in its surface area, would be no more than a pocket handkerchief: the North with its snow, bordering on Canada; the South with constant heat in Florida—at Miami—palm trees and resort cities and water sports; New Orleans with its Negroes and the busy shipping of the Mississippi. Then the expanses of grain extending as far as the eye can see to the foot of the Rocky Mountains. The canyons. Finally, at the very end, their paradise: California and the access to the Pacific, the islands, Tahiti, and new amusements. China faces them. Americans are thoroughly comfortable in their colonial style cottages—an architecture of high quality which expresses a healthy spirit, an ample and reasonable life.

New York, they feel, is a little bit diabolical. New York is not American. It is a world capital and has no frontier. I myself have the right to become a New Yorker, if I am strong enough to cut a furrow in New York. I should not thereby become an American!

For a traveler, New York is the great event of the journey. To penetrate American life—the real life—would require years —a genuine exploration. I am going to surprise you: Americans do not know America, the country is too large; they have neither the occasion nor the time, nor the means, nor any real reason to travel in their country. No more do the New Yorkers know New York. New York is too large and the day has only twenty-four hours. Travelers have a point of view about the city: we have come to see, to study, to understand, to judge. The average, ordinary life does not take up our attention. If the opportunity presented itself we could understand and enjoy the life of the cowboy on his ranch. We should find there a natural man, and that is the bottom of the question. In the innumerable cities of the USA we divine average societies in the process of development, on the long road of quality; the average, average situations

seem to us mediocre and they cannot hold our interest. What
we require is the potential which belongs to the *great cities*.
Drama, intensity, violence even, human substance—the human
quality which is unbridled here and which elsewhere, in the average cities, covers itself with shame. New York is a world capital
and has no shame. It is raw.

Whether it is in Chicago or in New York, you will be shown
only the handsome quarters; you will never be entertained except
by hosts in comfortable circumstances; very comfortable, terribly
comfortable in the midst of pathetic masses. The slums of Chicago are terrible. The slums are the tragic zones where there are
only hovels, lives crushed by the horror of the physical setting,
lodgings which are not just burrows but instruments of torture.
The slums are not simply physically ugly. Chicago, for instance,
offers a striking spectacle in Drexel Avenue which is composed
of private houses in the form of German Renaissance castles;
some years ago it was the center of high life. One day, as a result
of one of the violent shifts which are part of the destiny of cities
(Paris: Place des Vosges emptied to fill up the Faubourg Saint-
Germain; the boulevard of Saint Martin abandoned for the
Madeleine Boulevard; then, today, a great movement toward the
Champs Elysées and the creation of an important new center in
the west at the expense of the boulevards which have enjoyed
a hundred glorious years, etc. . . .), Chicago was cut in two:
the east-west axis of the city (like the Avenida de Mayo in
Buenos Aires) determined the destiny of two sections of the
city. The fashionable quarter was in the south; suddenly it
changed to the north. The southern part was abandoned. Who
will live in these princely (and dubious) residences on Drexel
Avenue? No one. Nevertheless, after a certain amount of time,
the Negroes take it over. They settle down behind broken windows covered over by boards; a villa becomes a village; there are
weeds in the rubbish-filled gardens, behind rusting iron fences.
There is misery there. For whoever says Negro in the USA says
pariah. This slum, then, is sinister not because of the place itself

but because of the kind of spirit which has sown death in this former "paradise." But there are slums in all the horror of the word: shanties of wood and blackened brick which show a neglect, a disintegration, a complete decay of that sign of vitality: maintenance. They wring your heart. They are new slums. They are from twenty to fifty years old. The tuberculous blocks in Paris, the Barrio Chino in Barcelona (a center of prostitution), are an admission that misery is the normal lot of the cadavers of cities, of the putrefying sections of the city. It is a tragic sign of decadence: it means that something has gone wrong with the social machine, it is an accusing witness of the times which have allowed some members of society to rot for the sake of loading other, privileged persons with jewels, rings, rivers of pearls and diamonds.

I scarcely more than glimpsed the slums of New York and I believe that New Yorkers never see them in their daily rounds; they are unaware of them. If they knew the slums, it would make them sick at heart and they would make new city plans. For the world needs city planning in order to conquer human misery.

For instance, in the "moral" slums of Chicago I noticed this: laboring men and office workers are obliged to travel more than fifty miles a day in streetcars and buses in order to earn their living!

From a plane you can grasp more clearly the wretchedness of urban agglomerations and particularly the calamity in the lives of millions of Americans who are thrust into the purgatory of the transportation system. You get the idea of catastrophe, urban catastrophe—the harassed life of men, women, and children; the sections in which human wastes stagnate—the poor devils so battered by their situation that they do not have the mind, the strength, the power, or the means to get together and cry halt. The national leaders and the city fathers are unconscious of *the reality of their misery*. After a stimulating cocktail they pass through the golden portals of Grand Central Terminal into a Pullman which takes them to their car; after a ride along charming country roads they enter the quiet and delightful living rooms of their colonial style houses.

Americans are eminently democratic—except about Negroes and that is a very grave question which cannot be resolved in a superficial way—they are good-natured, cordial, and companionable. The misery of our times comes from the fact that those who rule are those who have succeeded and who, consequently and quite naturally, live in conditions of material well-being. Inevitably, in spite of themselves and despite an evident good will, they are ignorant of the great charnel house of human misery. The day is only twenty-four hours long and each morning one must take up again the task left behind the evening before; it is a tiring job; thus the circuit closes, tightly, automatically. One cannot bring accusations against those who have succeeded for surrounding themselves with gracious things and thus losing sight of the urban catastrophe.

Moreover, New York is fascinating because of the other catastrophe, the fairy catastrophe: Manhattan, a city of skyscrapers, a vertical city.

The island is spread out like a sole in the water of the Hudson and East rivers. The fins along the two flanks represent the most perfect disposition of forms for a mercantile port. When you see it from a plane you think: Manhattan is a type-area for a modern city; the range of banks sheltered from the sea has the purity of a theorem. But now look at it on foot, along the avenue which skirts the river; the docks and ships form the teeth of a comb as far as you can see. The arrangement is clear, logical, perfect; nevertheless, it is hideous, badly done, and incongruous; the eye and the spirit are saddened. What could have been a communal enterprise, ordered in a serene and monumental unity, what could have been an endless jewel case for those marvels: liners or freighters—everything lacks order, everything has been badly constructed in the worst parts and even in the best ones. It was done by rapacious money-grubbers. This fringe along the water, around the whole periphery of Manhattan, is nothing but dirty scum. Nevertheless, necessity has already forced a fresh start. Since nothing had been conceived systematically, it had not been possible to look ahead. Along this too narrow waterfront avenue —which is supposed to serve two opposed purposes: as an artery for easy circulation, and as the location of quiet basins for loading and unloading—there exists the most complete confusion. You should watch a liner unload or take on passengers with their trunks. It is an edifying sight! What a wretched business! You get by of course! Will contemporary society then go on forever in the chaos of an everlasting getting by? Will getting by be our only discipline? What a failure and what a shameful opportunity is afforded those who are unscrupulous or overcunning! Since the avenue on the river was bottled up and unusable, it was decided to construct the saving instrument of all modern city planning: the highway on piles, in the air, free, connected with the ground by ramps at appropriate intervals—the highway on which cars can travel at full speed. Above the hell of traffic, you leap forward, you escape into a real joyousness by means of the elevated highway: you see the ships, the water, the sky-scrapers, the sky; you are free!

Ah! if the docks could be done over again, reconstructed in a unified way! Docks are hangars; there is no mystery about that, nor any secret of construction. Encircling all of Manhattan, more than twenty miles, pure and splendid docks would form a neck-lace of useful architecture around the city. It would be both efficient and profitable. My hand trembles, I am tempted to pick up a pencil. It would be so easy to do it well. That single project would illustrate the benefits of communal enterprise. Blind and self-seeking men have spoiled everything!

Within the ring of its docks Manhattan thrusts itself up into the sky. A great many skyscrapers fill the space, shut off the horizon. I did not imagine that there were so many of them; I imagined a few examples of boldness and vanity. But the whole city is vertical—or at least it seems to be, for a limited number of verticals succeed in taking up the blue of the sky.

It must be said that here the skyscrapers are an architectural accident. Imagine a man undergoing a mysterious disturbance of his organic life: the torso remains normal, but his legs become ten or twenty times too long. Thus the torso of normal houses set in normal plots of ground has suddenly been raised up on an unexpected support. They have become lost in an abstract tangle of calculations. As a result of paper calculations and new methods of construction, stimulated by somewhat unreasonable considerations, they have ignored the contingencies and plunged themselves into the unknown: three hundred feet, six hundred feet, a thousand feet. . . .

The former contingencies remain and the result has been catastrophe.

The torsos of buildings were pierced with windows; the disproportionately large supports also. I have already mentioned the cottage or private-house windows, the traditional windows which belong to the period of heavy walls of brick or stone. Anachronistic windows which nevertheless have one virtue—they express the presence of a normal man, a man behind an old-fashioned window. Thus punctuating the blue sky in a very simple, regular, and automatic way—yes, a fatal and indisputable way—there are now in the sky hundreds of thousands of windows, perhaps millions. It is very moving. Mediocre and retrograde poets who write about sunsets falling on old stones, you deny that man— good-natured man, with two feet, a head, and a heart—is an ant or a bee subject to the necessity of living in a box, a case, behind a window; you ask for a complete freedom, a complete fantasy, in accordance with which everyone would act in his own fashion, carried along by a creative lyricism in ever-new paths, never beaten paths, but individual ones, various, unexpected, extemporized, endlessly fanciful. Well, here is the proof that a man holds fast to the box which is his room; and a window opens on the outside world. It is a law of human biology; the square case, the room is a useful creation, proper to human beings. The window behind which a man stands is a poem of intimacy, of the free consideration of things. A million windows in the blue sky. The fairylike atmosphere begins with them.

A hundred times I have thought: New York is a catastrophe, and fifty times: it is a beautiful catastrophe.

One evening about six o'clock I had cocktails with James Johnson Sweeney—a friend who lives in an apartment house east of Central Park, over toward the East River; he is on the top floor, one hundred and sixty feet above the street; after having looked out the windows, we went outside on the balcony, and finally we climbed up on the roof.

The night was dark, the air dry and cold. The whole city was lighted up. If you have not seen it, you cannot know or imagine what it is like. You must have had it sweep over you. Then you begin to understand why Americans have become proud of themselves in the last twenty years and why they raise their voices in the world and why they are impatient when they come to our country. The sky is decked out. It is a Milky Way come down to earth; you are in it. Each window, each person, is a light in the sky. At the same time a perspective is established by the arrangement of the thousand lights of each sky-scraper; it forms itself more in your mind than in the darkness perforated by illimitable fires. The stars are part of it also—the real stars—but sparkling quietly in the distance. Splendor, scintillation, promise, proof, act of faith, etc. Feeling comes into play; the action of the heart is released; crescendo, allegro, fortissimo. We are charged with feeling, we are intoxicated; legs strengthened, chest expanded, eager for action, we are filled with a great confidence.

That is the Manhattan of vehement silhouettes. Those are the verities of technique, which is the springboard of lyricism. The fields of water, the railroads, the planes, the stars, and the vertical city with its unimaginable diamonds. Everything is there, and it is real.

The nineteenth century covered the earth with ugly and soulless works. Bestiality of money. The twentieth century aspires to grace, suppleness. The catastrophe is before us in the darkness, a spectacle young and new. The night effaces a thousand objects of debate and mental reservation. What is here then is true! Then everything is possible. Let the human be written into this by conscious intention, let joy be brought into the city by means of wisely conceived urban machinery and by generous thinking, aware of human misery. Let order reign.

In the store windows I saw an album published for the Christmas season by Scribner's: *The Magical City*. I reflect and argue with myself. I change it to: *The Fairy Catastrophe*. That is the phrase that expresses my emotion and rings within me in the stormy debate which has not stopped tormenting me for fifty days: hate and love.

For me the fairy catastrophe is the lever of hope.

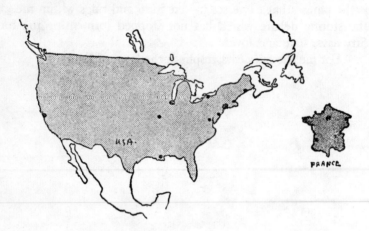

YOU ARE STRONG

You are strong in the USA!

This remains to us: we have reflected and have perhaps discovered the philosophy of things. Let's work together. Let's throw a bridge across the Atlantic. New York is the city nearest to Paris: first a train ride from Paris to Le Havre. Then the ship.

The ship is a place of repose, of preparation, of incubation. It is a delightful life. It's hardly a journey. It's a period of leisure. Thus, for instance, the three nights and two days on the train to Moscow are, on the contrary, a severe trial. The ship is a joy. Some day steamship companies will realize that ships can be made which are not imitations of palaces on land. I said to M. Vilars, the expert and affable purser of the *Normandie*, "The *Normandie* is a magnificent ship. In itself it is a success; there is nothing to criticize." But some day I hope to collaborate in the planning of a *tonic steamship*, a ship on which you do not dissipate a week in the midst of Capuan delights, but on which you use your time; where you feel yourself on the sea, where etiquette is banished or at least has got rid of the vestiges of past times. The ship would be transparent, you would always see the ocean; from every part. For, in the *Normandie*, you don't suspect for a minute that you are at sea; you have to go on deck to look for the sea. The main deck is not very helpful: it is a covered walk barricaded by thick wooden panels. There should be a number of swimming pools which are not studiously "decorative," race tracks, opportunities to climb up and down. It should be possible to see the superb machinery by means of properly arranged mirrors. There should be available popularizing marine instruments which would allow some participation in the activities of the bridge. Sports clothes, an ambient stimulated by the purser, an ambient of activity and not of cocktails. An informal ballroom. A library which would enable you to enter into marine interests: voyages, adventures, ship building, conquests. Public rooms and cabins done in nautical architecture and not by "interior decorators." Why this dissimulation, this equivocation, this hypocrisy through which the passenger is made to feel that he is still in the Place de l'Opéra or at Vichy? Is it an attempt to keep him from being seasick? I am persuaded that the effect is just the contrary: when the Louis XVI pilasters slant at an angle of thirty degrees, I consider that the "customer" has a right to be disturbed; it is worse than an earthquake. But

if his architectural setting were made up of the same elements
that establish the splendor of the hull, the limpidity of the
bridges, the rationality of the rigging and the machines, I think
that the hiatus would be less shocking; it would not exist. The
mobility which is the very essence of a ship would become normal and harmonious; anxiety would not arise, or at least the
architectural frame would not be contributory to the anxiety.
The only time that I have been seasick was in 1896, at the "Palace of Fairies," at a fair when I was a child; you entered a room
treated in the academic architectural way, and decorated by
hangings. There were at least forty of us. Then, though the floor
on which we were seated remained stationary, a mechanism
caused the walls and ceiling to see-saw; the architecture seemed
to be turned upside down, the columns leaned over frightfully
. . . and seasickness attacked us.

If the "tonic steamship" existed—with its sea air, whipping
winds or storms, sun, movement, promenades, swimming, racing
and training, visual pleasure in the marine views, etc. . . . the
crossing from Le Havre to New York, as a result of this strata-
gem, would be, in effect, no more than a trip to the gates of
Paris. No longer would the skyscrapers make our trumped-up
Louis XVI style look silly. We would enter into the spirit of the
city quite readily and we would speak to Americans not of "our
traditional, historic, and exquisite taste," but of the things which
trouble them and the things to which they aspire: wise conceptions of life. And, also, our celebrated "measure" would not be
an eternal restriction, but an active thing: "You are strong, but
we have reflected. . . ."

PRIDE

In the period after World War I America entered into the
life of the world. New York is a universal city, the first city to
be constructed on the scale of modern times. And in their hearts
Americans are proud. They represent a very special psychological
case: there is a great affection for the countries of their origin—
England, Germany, Italy, France, Spain, Russia, etc.; a great
anxiety in feeling themselves so suddenly placed on top of the
world; a need to add years to their life, the illusion of faraway
years. And they surround themselves with a ritual setting of
buildings and furniture of former times (the case of the universities with their reconstructions of Gothic times, as exquisite as
they are laughable, is typical). Finally, since Manhattan is up-
right in the sky, a lasting pride.

They are extraordinarily cordial; they extend their hands to
you in a strong, frank way. But if you express great admiration,
you will overwhelm them. And since their course is so different
from ours, so strong, so full of explosive power, their work gigantic already; and since it looms up gigantically before them
in the future, in their hearts they no longer feel that they are
"immigrants" from over there, colonists, uprooted people. The
USA has grown up; its shoulders are formidable, its animating
breath powerful. What are we in our flat cities? What is our
response to the skyscrapers of Manhattan? Versailles and Fon-
tainebleau, Touraine with Chenonceaux and Chambord? They
came to study all that at the Ecole des Beaux-Arts in Paris, and
they have made skyscrapers out of them! If that represents, with
us, an indisputable moral grandeur, is it not that of times which
are past? Inside themselves they think: What are you doing
today with your traditions of grandeur? Mean things. That is a

quite new feeling, for the USA, first among us, has passed on with a bound to the scale of modern times.

And now that this high level of moral satisfaction has been reached, they insist on re-establishing the steps leading up to it: inventory, archives, or genealogical tree. "It would be a good thing if a history of the United States were to fall into your hands. You would find in it the reasons for our thoughts and actions"—a somewhat mocking kind of security.

It would not be necessary—that would cause an unfortunate split—that this quite legitimate feeling should join hands with the feeling which prepared the German attack of 1914. At that time, in Cologne during July, at the end of the Werkbund Congress, I heard one of the great socialist orators of the Reichstag exclaim: "Now let Germany embark on the conquest of the world and bring about the triumph of German taste. . . ."

This clearly bellicose cry shocked us; but our cathedrals were no longer white. Our good taste, pinned up on the national coat of arms, was only the end of a heritage. Is not the same "good taste" expressed in the accumulation of rubbish which today blocks all our paths? At a dinner with four hundred architects in New York, after the talks were over, I met a distinguished gentleman with a white mustache. "I am French," he told me, "and an architect. I am no longer a practicing architect; I am a professor of architecture at New York University. I teach my students good taste and beauty." I replied: "Fine, but there are a good many things to say about that subject." The remark struck me as droll. I inquire about him. It turns out that this amiable man is an implacable enemy of everything new. Learning that there was a plan to bring me to the USA, he said "No" when he was asked whether it was worthwhile.

That kind of good taste is failing in America. It was in favor before the war. Now we are faced with a phenomenal American development, and the USA is no longer the purchaser of "French good taste." Later on I shall show that today the USA buys the French taste of creators, of inventors, of people who have faith:

all the production dishonored by our Academy, boycotted by our Ecole des Beaux-Arts.

No doubt that traditional good taste made Americans consider us good talkers, witty, and apt at doing Regency or Louis XV pirouettes, and some people in the USA, with a pride that puts us in our place, conclude: "You are Latins, we are Anglo-Saxons." We have not won that game. Henceforth it is only on the terrain of the new times that we can make our voices heard in New York.

The important man, a true transatlantic gentleman, with whom I was in constant contact during my American tour, still writes to me: "Our divergences are summed up in a difference of race. Good common sense is a negligible quantity for you and the call of glory leaves me cold. That is the difference between Latins and Anglo-Saxons. . . ."

A quick resolution of a question which deserves examination and which demands a categorical amendment. The Latins also practice good old common sense, alas! There is M. Clement Vautel—the "discourager"—enjoyed by innumerable Frenchmen in this depressing period of inertia, disillusionment, and apprehension. All the same the Frenchman has the historic virtue of practicing plain common sense. I have attended a great many international meetings. They are extremely confused and it is the Frenchman who puts them in order again, quickly, cleanly, clearly. One of the things which struck me in the USA was the slowness, the tergiversation, the uncertainty, the prolongation of every discussion which was supposed to lead to a decision. And that for the smallest things in life, in the matter of an ordinary appointment to be decided upon. It made me nervous. Other French people in New York and Chicago confirmed my opinion. If need be good old common sense may prevail in "business." And yet I have a vague feeling that Americans play hard in business; I even have the feeling that their minds apply themselves intensely to money questions. The rule of money is strong; it absorbs an infinite amount of energy. If the skyscrapers are constructed wonderfully fast, in the record time of one or two years, complete, equipped, exactly on schedule, it is not the result of a shattering rapidity of mind; it is simply the imperative law of money which mobilizes energies as if in the midst of a battlefield. Time is money. And meanwhile torrents, Niagaras of shares pour out in urgent waves and speed is only a function of big investments.

We are accused of loving glory, a truism which was fabricated abroad. If the sword was directed at me, it is blunted by a blow on my armor of indifference. I am a little bit of an annoyance to journalists, who do their duty of course, but thoroughly bore me: I receive them without a smile. But in America glory is such a coveted commodity that journalism, and especially publicity, play an immense role. Over there it is something ineffable to have your name printed or your photograph reproduced a million times. The sacred ritual was followed in my case. A director of publicity at the Museum of Modern Art concerned herself with me. When I returned to New York a month later I was told: "There are almost four hundred articles about you in the library." I replied: "Very well, very well."—"But aren't you going to read them, take them with you?"—"No, miss, I don't even wish to see them."

Such a response is a *casus belli*: an offense to the goddess Publicity.

If I very much hope that my friend will not allow us any "good common sense" (it is too fine a dream), on the basis of this first experience of America I ask at least the acceptance as valid of our own *bon sens*, a Latin quality. I am by no means saying that we are the exclusive possessors of it, but the American phenomenon in its gigantism appears to us lacking in good sense in many spectacular manifestations.

Glory? Well, before this controversy was born, following the letter mentioned above, I had already explained that it leaps up toward the sky from Manhattan, in plumes. "Your skyscrapers are too small and they are not rational," that was also a *casus belli*.

The Museum of Modern Art presented a large exhibition of modern painting, from Cézanne up to the present, painting from Paris, since Paris is still the nurse of the arts. My friend La Roche has the finest collection of cubist painting in his house at Auteuil: Picasso, Braque, Léger, Gris. The museum asked him to lend some of his best pieces. La Roche replied: "Gladly; but since the depression has spread misery in the world of the arts, I wish to establish a small relief fund—it is a modest initiative of my own—and I leave it to the Museum to decide the amount of its contribution to this necessary fund." The Museum (Rockefeller Foundation) replied: "Our means do not permit us . . . but on the other hand your artists will receive magnificent publicity and France will be honored." La Roche telegraphed: "A thousand regrets, my pictures will not cross the ocean!" In the USA I got tired of hearing about the taste for glory. Here is what explains the whole thing: over there glory is useful. It makes the product known, it brings in money. And that is why I believe that, far from being nonexistent in the USA, on the contrary glory and good common sense are Siamese twins.

Nevertheless it must be admitted that the truism which brings us sly criticism from abroad has an origin. Our press flatters our vanity. No sensational discovery is made in America, in Russia, in Germany, or in Kamchatka which does not have its fatal explanation: "Yes, but . . . that was discovered long ago, by a Frenchman. . . ." It is often true. What is nearly always true is that that Frenchman almost starved to death. It is a frequent and regular story. In general, journalists mention him without comment. Americans then could say more justly: "Glory is a good patron of the House of France, but the House of France does not serve either food or drink; on the other hand, it offers fine discourses later on, at the fiftieth anniversary of the death of its great men."

IS IT A CANCER?

American advertising is a kind of narcissism. A man is a
company and a company is a poster, a gag in a magazine, an
immense colored billboard set up in the country at a crossroad.
The area is so large that it is necessary to inform its one hundred
and forty million inhabitants, in the city and in the country, that
this or that exists. Such is the healthy origin of advertising.

Consider it in its effects. What I shall say about it also concerns European countries, but in an infinitely lesser degree. The
country is made up of two flocks of sheep, facing each other,
head against head and pushing against each other with all their
strength. Result: almost complete immobility for a maximum of
effort! I sponsor a product; in the office of a skyscraper a type-
writer pounds away; at the printer's machines vomit up torrents
of leaflets. Immediately, in another skyscraper, another type-
writer taps out the antiproduct, the rival; from another press
comes a second flood of leaflets. It is a question of winning out!
Ingenuity, clever or crude ideas, cries into the face of the country. My clamor must not be drowned out. And the other company begins to make more noise. So it goes. The newspapers take
on unheard-of proportions; and the magazines? Well, the intellectual matter is often thin, but on the other hand the pages of
advertising multiply in an extraordinary way. Americans say to
us: "I think our advertising is remarkable; I take a keen pleasure
in it. I am amused by reading proclamations and replies. It is
really stimulating."

There is in it, in its enormity, a disproportion of effort. Too
much energy, too much money (and consequently too much
energy again) are swallowed up in the scramble. Study the economy of the country: careful statistics could show the cost. That
expenditure is not used to produce consumption goods, but sim-

ply to send cries across the countryside. All that money represents hours of work, work turned into noise and wind. Those
sterile labors eat into the economy of the country. Those fruitless
labors are the hours of daily work devoted to paying for that
noise and wind. An hour a day from the mass of the people?
Perhaps. Later on I shall speak of the three hours used up daily
by Americans traveling in cars, trolleys, or subways; and then
the four hours (possibly) devoted to paying for the immense,
colossal, frightening waste of garden cities or distended urban
agglomerations. Add it up: one, plus three, plus four; there are
eight hours lost each day by vast numbers of people. It was
hardly worth while to free the Negroes in the 1860's, since there
are dreadful new hidden chains which fetter life to the point of
breaking the family cell: American hard work, their effervescence,
the fabulous machinery of skyscrapers, telephones, the press, all
of that is used to produce wind and to chain men to a hard
destiny.

If I were in authority, I would forbid advertising. But I
would issue classified catalogues of production. And ingenuity
would be used to present the clearest and most precise explanation of the object offered for sale. Nothing else. Extravagant
claims for foods or aids to digestion would be prohibited. Companies would sell more. The market would be more certain,
charlatans put out of business.

The deluge of advertising would be too much for me: the
traffic lights cause vertigo; in the streets and along highways immense, shining, and as it were cellophaned, posters—young men
and young women of the pure American type, exuberantly
healthy, their cheeks provided with useful reflections—fruits
shining and also cellophaned, with all their reflections; boxes of
various products, bottles, cars, always cellophaned and supplied
with reflections. . . . M. Ingres, raising his finger, said to his
students: "Gentlemen, reflections are unworthy of great art."

American advertising lacks charm and interest. Not very
lively, not brisk, it is without plastic quality. This will disappoint

Americans. Well, we have been spoiled in Paris since 1890. Sometimes we see posters which are masterpieces of wit and plasticity: a true patrimony. Sometimes we cry: "Bravo!" for the walls decorated by those remarkable frescoes. The poisoning of the city and rural areas by distressing, insistent billboards should not be allowed! At least wit should have a place in it somewhere.

But on the other hand I cannot pass by the luminous advertising on Broadway. Everyone has heard about that incandescent path cutting diagonally across Manhattan in which the mob of idlers and patrons of motion pictures, burlesque shows and theaters moves. Electricity reigns, but it is dynamic here, exploding, moving, sparkling, with lights turning white, blue, red, green, yellow. The things behind it are disappointing. These close-range constellations, this Milky Way in which you are carried along, lead to objects of enjoyment which are often mediocre. So much the worse for advertising! There remains a nocturnal festival characteristic of modern times. I remember that the light filled our hearts, and that the intense, powerful color excited us and gave us pleasure. And on Broadway, divided by feelings of melancholy and lively gaiety, I wander along in a hopeless search for an intelligent burlesque show in which the nude white bodies of beautiful women will spring up in witty flashes under the paradisaic illumination of the spotlights.

A BUSINESS LUNCH AT THE PLAZA

Habits delineate the character of countries.

Through a long tradition of cooking, through the wise design of meals, through the effect of wine, man's good companion, the Frenchman has learned how to eat and how to act at table. Meals are still among the good moments of life, thank God. French people talk when they are eating; conversation is a sign of culture. Business matters are forgotten; men and women enjoy their taste for companionship. Those who have traveled have noticed that some peoples do not talk while they are eating. On this side or on that side of frontiers dining rooms are either silent or resound with bons mots and ideas. American restaurants are devoid of conversation.

I note this characteristic thing: the café terrace is Latin. London, New York, Berlin, Vienna, Moscow, do not have them. The apéritif hour is Latin. In New York it is the cocktail hour.

You have cocktails at the homes of various friends after your day's work in the city. Thirty people, fifty people, even more. You stand up. It is impossible to carry on a conversation standing up, for, in the middle of a phrase, a third person intervenes, taps you on the shoulder and says "Hello!" It is useless to go on trying, conversation is out of the question. One cocktail leads to another, your blood warms up, voices rise; the noise, annoying at first, becomes intolerable. Everyone shouts and has an alcoholic smile. Cudgel blows on spirits wearied by hard work in the city. Decidedly, conversation is impossible.

A French apéritif is taken when you are seated around a table. There are two, three, four persons. You have chosen your companions. You drink slowly. Conversation is calm, interrupted by the silences of well-being: you talk, you discuss, you can even enter into disputes. But the idea is followed through. Thus personal ideas are born, points of view, opinions. It is an agora around a siphon. The apéritif is a social institution and the café terrace is an urban institution. I may say, at the end of this panegyric, that I do not take apéritifs, since I lack the time.

The business lunch took place at the Plaza, an excellent first-class hotel of the old type. I like those vast and handsome hotels which are not at all in modern style but which have acquired a past through their richness and substantiality. There are living pasts and dead pasts. Some pasts are the liveliest instigators of the present and the best springboards into the future. Here it is simply the past of substantial times.

A French steel magnate introduced us to the president and vice-president of one of the five greatest companies of the world. Introduction, cocktails while the hors d'oeuvres are being served. In a few precise words he explains the purpose of our meeting. Immediately I submit my proposals. The back of the menu serves for graphic illustrations whose eloquence avoids the ambushes of language. Questions, replies. It is finished in a quarter of an hour. Everything is quite clear, understood, and the order of operations decided upon. Then my friend begins to talk again. He is telling a story. The eyes of the guests express attention, they smile, then come stupefaction, embarrassment, finally a great burst of laughter. They have just heard a good joke, a Gallic back-room story, something terribly crude and droll. They are put at ease, and the lunch made cheerful. Business matters are put aside, forgotten. Appetite comes with talk. We leave each other without formality, in friendship, in comradeship. Wit purged us of business preoccupations. Thenceforth a kind of complicity exists among us. A gay lunch facilitates business transactions.

A BUSINESSMEN'S DINNER IN BOSTON

Today I am dining alone at the Copley-Plaza in Boston. I am bored and have time to observe. In the dining room of this excellent hotel there is a religious silence. Opposite me are three men who are certainly engineers. Every five minutes one of them speaks. Silence and mastication. The three men have handsome heads, characteristic of their country: balanced, strong, energetic. One is old, one young, one middle-aged. The meal is finished. Coffee. Silence. Then after a long time conversation begins. Unquestionably they are talking about their discoveries, but without passion or excitement. They masticate their words, speak quietly and reflectively. I should even say that they seem as if they were under the influence of a religious event. Those men won me with their handsome faces. I think: what a grave and serious country! When such men take hold of an idea or begin to act, they do not let go. But, on the other hand, if they are undoubtedly happy in their serenity, they have not yet tasted the joys of thought—not of thought which is a line of conduct, an ethic (they certainly have that), but of active, ardent thought, which contains the joys of a profusely flowered field.

Several days previously some New York engineers had given a lunch for me at their club. Observations of the same sort. Considering their look, I notice once more the presence of the sexual question. Their eyes are striking.

Relations of men and women. Engineers at work, "hard labor" in the business community, the urban crime of frightfully extended city regions. Life injured every day by the unbalance of machine age times. I begin to put my reflections together: the core of the family is affected. Americans who live in cities often say: "We are victims of an inferiority complex. . . ." Thus those thousand-foot skyscrapers!

The end of our meal was calm, silent, meditative, each one
bearing within himself a perhaps maladjusted heart.

THE INDIAN RAIDS ARE NOT FAR AWAY

I have a grudge against modern papers and especially American papers. A triumph of invention and energy enables us to
keep informed about world events hour by hour. We could have
the chart of the world's palpitation printed in black and white
for a trifling sum. A short and faithful paper. But not at all: the
paper is immense and it "arranges" the truth! The Sunday New
York Times weighs more than two and a half pounds. Note the
weight. It contains a few decigrams of excellent, well-presented
ideas, first-class information.

And the rest! Advertising and news about gangsters. In addition, numerous pictorial supplements designed to pass away the
time, to take up time. That is precisely what I have against
present-day papers. I make the point and admit that it is one of
the fatalities of our epoch; being a city planner, I understand:
what do you expect so many million people to do, divided as
they are by the choice between their mediocre apartments and
the far from attractive streets? The weight of the modern paper,
then, is a direct function of urban discomfort.

French papers, relatively brief, well-organized, skillfully balance the doses of serious things—politics and economics, and
"exciting" things—housekeepers' stories: revolvers, women cut
in two, scabrous trials. I do not dislike these housekeepers' tales.

Their cardinal virtue is *being true*. They touch the depths of human psychology, are everyday Balzac. Balzac often did not dare to risk anything as strong as life, as it is reported in the papers. "I should remain plausible," he said. The paper is often *incredible*; it is not useless to learn what life is like. It is well to be informed and to know that there are wolves on the steppes.

The papers in America are filled with stories about crime. There are still quite a few gangsters. In fact, the gangster is a natural American product: the Indian raids are not far away.

Broadway has the feeling of gangsterdom in its intrusive mixture of alert crooks and honest visitors in search of slightly equivocal sensations. Broadway, world-known, is stretched out like a tightrope on which there is an abundance of dancers. Along it you see the confusion of disembarkation, the recent unpacking of a civilization. An intensely living place, very "new world."

The colonists—for there actually are colonists and the American spirit itself is strongly marked by the disciplines and irruptions of a society which in a sense has just disembarked, attracted by violently opposed motives: some wishing to save and maintain their faith, their religion, or their ethical attitude; others eager for adventures, for deeds, for money-making—the colonists are renewed every day. People from the interior of the country, who have come on some business pretext, cannot really go elsewhere, for Broadway is the street of welcome: the cataracts of light which they have seen in the movies and read about in the papers have drawn them for a long time. The places of entertainment and the displays of goods for out-of-town visitors are there. It is the complement of the plains and the cornfields. On a gigantic scale, Broadway is one of those general stores that you see along the new roads in Morocco or in the interior of the USA; assortments of wares where you find whatever is useful: nails, string, shirts, and somewhat gaudy ties, shoes, and in this case, in place of finding them in red-light districts, pretty girls in burlesque shows. Eating places along the way: supplies and passions, suspenders and girls, useful things and sexual excitement. The dream materialized here in a burst of light, of milling crowds, of carouses well framed by the glitter of chrome metal, brings to life again the great adventure of *The 8:47 Train* . . . on the scale of Manhattan.

CRESCENDO

The *Normandie* was an ambassador of France in America. The dimensions are not those of France, but those of America. The sea no longer exists; it is a transport casket. It is admirable— charm, easy and placid life. I think of my "tonic steamship." On board I asked the purser for dinner clothes with some color: the stewards dressed in vermilion are in keeping with the pomp of the ship; at dinner the rest of us are like people at a country funeral; the beautiful women seem like flowers in the splendors of their gowns. It is a curious end-result of civilization that men, who used to wear ostrich plumes on their heads, rose, white, and royal blue, a vesture of brocades or shimmering silk, should no longer know how to do anything but thrust their hands into the pockets of black trousers. Ten years ago Maurice de Waleffe felt this decadence; but his crusade broke its nose on silk stockings and shoes with incongruous buckles. The question has to be reconsidered and the transformation of masculine costume is necessary. It is as difficult as changing the ethics and the institutional state of a society. Costume is the expression of a civilization. Costume reveals the most fundamental feelings; through it we show our dignity, our distinction, our frivolity, or our basic ambitions. Though standardized, masculine dress does not escape individual decision. But it is no longer suitable. From what persists, we have proof that the machine age revolution has not reached maturity.

America knew about and had a malicious belief in the vibrations of the *Normandie*: "Were you very uncomfortable?"— "No, not at all! The vibrations of the *Normandie* are localized in the stern; four-fifths of the boat is free of them."—"Really? There is a woman who has been in the hospital for four months getting over the effects!" How all-powerful are the forces of prejudice! A technical masterpiece has been achieved; in her mind a woman has been made ill for months and Americans are delighted. Nevertheless, the *Normandie* (rightly or wrongly—I am neither a mariner nor a guardian of the French Treasury) was constructed on an American scale.

We saw the mystic city of the new world appear far away, rising up from Manhattan. It passed before us at close range: a spectacle of brutality and savagery. In contrast to our hopes the skyscrapers were not made of glass, but of tiara-crowned masses of stone. They carry up a thousand feet in the sky, a completely new and prodigious architectural event; with one stroke Europe is thrust aside, with its dimensions sophistically set by the resolutions of town councillors and "the force of our traditions."

For our benefit Manhattan repeats a lesson of natural history: man is an ant with precise habits of life, a unanimous mode of being. In wishing to "free" man from biological realities by an urban scheme spread over a vast area, our propagandists have plunged cities into the absurd, the backward, and into small enterprises which may compromise his health; the individual and the group are disturbed; mankind is disturbed.

From the first you feel that America is animated by an architectural spirit which is manifest in everything, skyscrapers, machines, objects, bars, clothes. There is a rich sense of things; it will develop between the impulses of will and power, between incontestable success and a funereal sadness which we shall speak about again.

Color enters in violently whenever money is involved. To call, you cry out; to cry out effectively in the uproar of the crowd, you use signs colored red, yellow, green, and blue. Magic incantation on Broadway. In the burlesques women with dazzling skin have golden locks, like metal chiseled by a goldsmith, with the vividness of something cut by a chisel. Incisive casques (not vaporous!), clean, curly, dense, lively, full in style. Along with that the woman is a healthy, beautiful animal, a very beautiful animal.

There is the sadness of strong-armed, full-hearted young men. Their spirits have not set out in search of the inner joys which are the fruit of civilization. They feel themselves empty. Troubled by the incapacity of their age—the age of the people— they are grieved and melancholy. Money is too important in America.

In the universities young men and young women seek knowledge and, some of them, wisdom.

It is there that the Frenchman triumphs. He no longer feels the anxieties of adolescence. France is grown-up. Travels in all countries attest the spiritual strength of Frenchmen. That has often been said and written. In the display of the virtues of the world the spiritual strength of the Frenchman makes its appearance. Far from being made a basis for vanity or inertia, on the contrary, in this perilous hour of history, that force should be seized, adjusted to the motor, and set in motion. Let the current be transmitted; let an unused virtue bear fruit; let a sleeping capital nourish the activities of the nation and more than that: let it bring its precious ferment into the symphony of peoples. Two thousand years of unbroken, uninterrupted experience cannot fall asleep at the decisive hour, or be put under a bushel, or shut up in jealous Bastiles by dotards who beat the air with their arms because a new world is breaking forth and a new civilization is beginning.

Thus, for instance, the museum in Hartford, Connecticut, a museum which is intensely alive, is essentially French (of the France which is dishonored by the France under the ferule of the Academies). The painter Fernand Léger has never been so well presented as he was at the Museum of Modern Art in New York. Later on I shall speak of the art of Paris which has conquered the whole world and which, in America, is shown with real solemnity: artists pilloried by the Institut de France and put on the auction block by the State. Rejection, refusal, that is the story of these last fifty years of servitude and catalepsy. One day, in South America, at Buenos Aires, an important person said to me: "You are acquainted with the ministers in Paris, tell them to stop taking us for idiots and to stop sending us their official lecturers and pictures and statues. France is disowned here. We know the true France!"

When the cathedrals were white, spirit was triumphant. But today the cathedrals of France are black and the spirit is bruised. The works of the new civilization are coming together in a symphonic crescendo. The guiding spirit is faltering. The young act, but they do not know. The old cling to their accumulated treasures, but are unable to accomplish anything further. The scale of the new enterprises makes itself visible in the modern world. Let the lightning flash spring up—union; let it break the narrow barriers; let it liberate all the repressed forces! Let suffocation be followed by flowering! Splendid and imminent adventure of a new Middle Ages.

In New York events have everywhere got ahead of the control of spirit. It is a titanic effort of organization and discipline in the midst of a chaos brought about by the speed of accelerated times: it is a kind of snorting monster, bursting with health, sprawled out at ease. There is a geometric progression of chaos. Encephalitis in the New York region: twelve million men dedicated to hard labor. In this hard reality there is no example for us to follow. It is an inundation. Wise views about a healthy life would be useful here. In this situation Cartesian reason could diagnose and suggest. I have a persistent feeling that France and America could exchange a solid handshake and do each other an infinite amount of good.

Thus this journey enables me to see clearly. In the USA I measure the effects of an ethic worthy of our sympathy: the quality of American workmanship. It appears in everyday matters, particularly in connection with comfort. It is the crown of mass production. When in 1920, in *l'Esprit Nouveau*, I wrote the chapter about the automobile and the Parthenon, in praise of *standardized things*, I astonished and even offended many perfumed hearts. In that case the discussion came before the reality; large-scale operation is indisputably the route to production and it leads to quality. Finally, this same element of workmanlike ethics still enters into the making of articles of luxury. We have too easily considered foreign production shoddy and we have not followed the march of the times which demanded that we give our designing and manufacturing groups machines capable of executing things better than they could be done by hand. *Machines which do things better than human hands* would not have paralyzed an imaginative and organizing spirit; they would have freed it and developed it tremendously. Thus, faced with markets which are collapsing everywhere, our awakening is bitter.

Back in Paris, I examine the urban scene with an avid curiosity. I am without prejudice. I feel certain solaces in Paris and how much disgust also. I notice that it is the finish of the houses and the details which have an architectural purpose (very much on the surface moreover) which make up an important part of the good breeding of the Paris street. *Sustained* comfort for the spirit, an *ambiance* of cleanness and solicitude in the service of excellence, from the ground to the top. The last well-bred houses belong to the period of Haussmann. Too often we forget to appreciate them.

We laugh at the crowns of New York skyscrapers which seem

like chased decanter stoppers. But how much more we should be distressed by the crowns of our own buildings constructed after 1900: those species of cupola installed (preferably) like a prow on the angle at a street intersection. And the architectural disaster brought about by a fatal regulation of setbacks? The great "Universal" or "International" exhibitions mark the face of the city with significant features. The basic evil is that exhibitions, which are interesting in periods of transition, try to compensate for the lack of a healthy and true program by spectacular manifestations. In a spirit of sham they construct buildings which have a sham purpose. It is sham because, with uncertainty in control, the officials timidly fall back on the provisional—the provisional, and plaster on a wooden framework. The sun and rain ruin the whole thing in six months: the pastries dissolve. O architecture, severe science of fruitful programs and of structures subjected to the laws of weight and to the specific virtues of matter! What backsliding! Decorations are made in that way. Decorations and not organisms. Decoration is the harbinger of fashions. The current fashion triumphs. The disaster is that in architects' offices the designers are won over to this specious attitude. Their hands and minds are warped. The effect cripples them and their work for twenty years. Moreover, the art(?) publishers do a lot of business: the world is flooded with albums of plates devoted to these unfortunate saturnalia. Cities and villas cover themselves with styles. "Styles!" Style of 1900, of 1925, etc.

And "my beautiful village," Paris, is blemished.

But the Paris of Henri IV (Pont-Neuf), of Louis XIV, of Louis XV, of Napoleon, shines with the brilliance of a lofty intention. The spirit which had given birth to the cathedral in the heart of the city had already been driven away. The individual had replaced the grandiose collectivity of the Middle Ages. A break had occurred at the time of the Renaissance. Bifurcation of destinies. That is the way it was, and it is useless to carp about it. Intention, at least, was still great and worthy and wished to set its works at the head of things then existing. Often for the sake of vanity, I admit.

Carrying within me the vision of Manhattan and the memory of the grandeur of American enterprises, for weeks in Paris I was like a fearful animal while re-establishing contact with this milieu that I loved so much, the memory of which had been brutally pushed aside by the clamor of the USA. Hate and love alternately in New York. Here also my heart knocks against the two poles of shame and delight. And I consider that Paris is good, not because of its dimensions, which are rather small, or at least medium, but through the harmony which exists in certain of its urban elements from the smallest detail (which counts, I feel that very clearly) to the limits of the ensemble against the sky. (Esplanade des Invalides.)

With Manhattan fixed in my memory, I feel that the new scale of enterprises which belongs to machine age society need bring no disturbance to the beauty of Paris; on the contrary: there is here, though it has been dormant for a long time, the sense of proportion which will master the new tasks and establish itself in the city in new and triumphant prisms.

L'ECOLE DES BEAUX-ARTS DE PARIS

"The Beaux-Arts School in Paris has done us harm here in the United States"—remark of a woman who is a professor of art history at Vassar.

The issue thus set forth fixes a point in the aesthetic and ethical history of the USA: henceforth America is going to de-

tach itself from the French influence embodied in that high institute of instruction: l'Ecole des Beaux-Arts. America is seeking its
own way, no longer has a blind respect for a once powerful idea.
The Association of those who possess diplomas from the French
Government will carry on until all its members are gone. An
Association bound together by good fellowship, happy memories, student epics (yes) . . . and one that has a flattering look:
the small vanity of belonging to this nobiliary group. Nevertheless, these French-trained men became Americans again a long
time ago, as their works show.

I do not intend to blame the Beaux-Arts School, but simply
to make an attempt to pose the problem of the School.

Schools are the product of nineteenth-century theories.
They have brought about immense progress in the domain of the
exact sciences; they have warped activities dependent on imagination, for they have fixed "canons," the "true" and "right"
rules, which are recognized, officially stamped, legally accepted.
In an epoch of total disorder in which nothing today is like
what it was yesterday, they have established an official break in
the form of a "diploma"; thus they are against life; they represent memory, security, lethargy. In particular, they have killed
architecture by operating in a vacuum, far away from the weight
of materials, the resistances of matter, the tremendous progress in
the field of machinery. They have vilified crafts associated with
matter, time, expense. Architecture has evaded life in place of
being an expression of it. The distressing ugliness of the nineteenth and twentieth centuries comes in a straight line from the
schools. This ugliness is not the result of bad intentions; on the
contrary it comes from incongruity, from incoherence, from the
separation which occurs between the idea and its realization. Design has killed architecture. Design is what they teach in the
schools. The leader of these regrettable practices, the Ecole des
Beaux-Arts in Paris, reigns in the midst of equivocation, endowed
with a dignity which is only a usurpation of the creative spirit of
earlier periods. It is the seat of a most disconcerting paradox,

since under the ferule of extremely conservative methods, everything is good will, hard work, faith. The dilemma is in the heart
of the School, an institution which is in excellent health, like
mistletoe that lives on the sap of dignified and lofty trees, like
cancer which establishes itself comfortably around the pylorus
of the stomach or around the heart. *The cancer is in excellent
health!* An image which can be extended to so many present-day
things in which through a frightening perversion of the powers
of life, life moves over into the camp of death and acts against
all its power. Death is in excellent health.

At the School the different camps are as clearly formed as
they are in the great events which today tear society apart. The
students are on one side, the masters on the other. The students,
naturally, ask only to be prepared for the radiant *tomorrow;* the
masters occupy a throne which they imagine they raised up;
from their heads nothing could come except infrangible truths;
they find certitude in this: what was yesterday has lived, has
existed, is therefore indisputable. Such is the material which
shall be taught. I would not be hostile to this method, having
applied it fully to everything which I have done since childhood,
if, in the case of the School, the commentary went thus: *"Here
is what was done; here are the reasons for it; in the present circumstances, such things can no longer be effective. On the other
hand, they show how, in all times and places, the spirit created,
made new things, marched forward solidly based on the existing
contingencies. Investigate the contingencies; establish their nature clearly and set your feet on that mobile springboard (how
new it is today) in order to leap forward. In that way you will do
things which are true, useful, and of unquestionable value."* Since
contingencies are often made up of new materials, revolutionary
techniques, entirely new programs, contact should be made with
crafts (materials and machines), with needs (a new society),
with the spirit (ethic of the new times). In contrast to that,
they have set up the design sheet as a method against the interests of architecture. Architecture is a putting in order; the opera-

tion takes place in your head; the sheet of paper will welcome only the technical signs which are useful in manifesting and transmitting the thought. Architecture can attain even lyricism; proportion is the means of architectural lyricism: volumes, cross section, surfaces, circulation, areas, contiguous elements, light. The design sheet will express itself in precise drawings which belong to the omnipresent field of mathematics. Architecture is the mold of a society; it constructs *shelters*. What is this society, then, and what are its needs? The design sheet will receive only what has been entrusted to it: the program itself. Architecture is a purely human creation. But since man is a product of nature, architecture will be a kind of logarithm of nature. Nature—its laws, its admirable principle and irrevocable organization, its classifications, its groups, its infinite diversity, its unitarian mathematics—will stamp its lesson in the heart of the architect and not in the washes of the design sheet. I admire the dazzling manual skill acquired by the students through the instruction of the Ecole des Beaux-Arts. . . . I could wish that the head might command the hand. I recognize the elegance which guides the solutions of plan, façade, and section. But I should like to see intelligence dominating elegance and not being disregarded. I regret that the problems at the School are conceived outside of the condition of the craft and that it does not call upon modern technicians except to accomplish miracles of bad quality: in order to make things stand up which, otherwise, could never be constructed or which would fall down if the materials shown in the design were used. In this matter modern times, with a fearful waste of money, is reduced to playing the role of prop for thought which lacks bones and muscles, for thought with its arm in a sling. Thus was born the architecture in a sling of the Ecole des Beaux-Arts.

I know quite well that later on, when the students are thrust into real life, they are forced to acquire a different diploma, a diploma without signatures or flattering emblems: that of reality. Some succeed very well; but the others are definitively "marked";

thenceforth the country is afflicted by their inauspicious activity for forty years. In New York I said to one of the School's students, winner of an American prize: "The instruction of the Ecole des Beaux-Arts allows the intelligent students to escape." He agreed with me enthusiastically.

I think that this kind of instruction, in the sumptuary form of a supreme diploma—coronation—organized, moreover, in the shadow of the Institute—is unacceptably pretentious in the midst of the great melee of modern times. Why should vanity be the appanage of the architect when architecture should never be vain, but healthy, just, and worthy? Besides, in the new times, architecture extends to the unprecedented mass of contemporary productions. Where does architecture belong? In everything! *Shelter*—dwellings and means of transportation (roads, railways, water, air). *Equipment*—the city, the farm, the useful village, the port, and also the furnishing of the house: domestic machinery. *Form*—everything that our hands touch or that our eyes see in this new world of materials and functional organisms which, in a hundred years, have so suddenly surrounded our life with plastic realities which are alive and palpitating in the light.

Shall we give, shall we demand diplomas for all the activities which have the right to relate themselves to architecture and which represent one of the largest parts of current activity? The world turned into diplomas? The question thus posed shows the ridiculousness of diplomas. We no longer need diplomas. The world is open, not closed.

The studious and painful conquest (I know that from the confidences of many young students) of the diploma demanded by the father or the family (poor people, they imagine that when their child leaves school he will be the beneficiary of exceptional rights in the apportionment of life), the winning of the diploma in four or six years absorbs the precious moments of youth, of generous malleability, of magnificent enthusiasm, of opening in the face of multifarious life. The diploma closes everything like a cork. It says: "It is finished, you have stopped suffering and learning. Henceforth you are free!" The idea of *learning* has become synonymous with *suffering!* Youth is killed. Learning? That is the joy of every day, the ray of sunlight in life. I say that if throughout life we developed the generous faculty of learning, men would discover in it happiness itself—free, unlimited, never-failing happiness, happiness up to their last day. We would make men of a different kind: new men.

In America a fork has appeared on the road of architecture. In a few years, and as a result of having built the skyscrapers (without conclusive results as yet), Americans have entered into the spirit of the times. In the colleges and universities (I shall speak of them at length), certain teachers see clearly and the students tremble with the sacred disquietude. Already the Ecole des Beaux-Arts has been thrust out of the intense life of America. Nevertheless, in many universities architectural instruction is still dull, flat, dreary, academic, so academic! Remember the deeply malignant statement of a professor at New York University which I have cited: "*I am no longer a practicing architect,* but I instruct my students in good taste and beauty." It was a man with a "diploma" who was speaking; a paper diploma was speaking, and not an architect. The diploma was glorified by the words: Diploma of the French Government.

In all humility I should like to know why the French Government considers itself authorized to give diplomas. I thought that the function of government was to administer its own times and to lead people on the paths of an ever-changing life; and not to set up obstacles.

When the cathedrals were white, there were no governmental diplomas; the crafts (and architecture) were practiced regionally in terms of local resources of raw materials, climates, customs. Controls were worked out in the midst of jobs to be done, through corporations. Those corporations were not "Institutes." Small groups of foremen and masters supported by the respectful esteem of their comrades, passed judgment on the technical qualities of the young. It was a living procedure, on a human scale. I repeat: the *control* was immediate. When things were centralized, then Parisianized, and when the Academies were founded, life retreated. It was put under cupolas—under dish-covers! The cathedrals were old, they even railed at them, they called them "Gothic" in order to indicate that they were barbarous. The corporations became academic. The Revolution destroyed them. With a laudable intention the national Schools were put in their place. It was an expedient, an organization which escaped the laws of human scale. The nineteenth century was to suffer as a result of it: ugliness, incoherence, and nonsense established themselves.

Architecture is in everything, it extends to everything. In the nature of things, small groups have recourse to direct, efficient instruction. A man can speak from his heart to young friends who come to bring him their collaboration, *through the truth of his work*, steeped in the realities of the present. It is the old workshop. Yes. Then it is a backward step? No, it is a return to human scale. It is good that open hearts bring their theoretical instruction to audiences and auditoriums. But let the craft be present at all times, from the first day, the true facts about technical methods, the real qualities of materials, the reality of the workyard. Scattered throughout the country there are men to whom the young will go when the country is reborn. They will be masters without titles or vanities, without wax seals, without fresh rubber stamps, without paraphernalia. They will teach youth that it must never stop learning.

4 SEARCHINGS AND MANIFESTATIONS OF THE SPIRIT

SEARCHINGS OF THE SPIRIT

It is here that the interesting articulation of the phenomenon called America is found. We are irritated, we are delighted. M. Duhamel, having visited the country with his eyes and heart closed, remained irritated. I think that the understanding of things comes through sympathy, a word which means that states of spirit touch each other. I feel sorry for the visitor, wherever he may be, who locks up his understanding in advance and only bothers himself about shaking the dust from his shoes.

This great people conquers and settles a vast territory; precisely during the machine age. It is composed of the stock of twenty races; it adopts a unique language which it speaks in its own way. The Anglo-Saxons dominated the others. Nevertheless, one nation has been formed: American. Today, after a century, the American and the Englishman are completely differentiated. Everything has led them to that result: the psychoethnic origins,

the work imposed by the problem of colonization, the absorp-
tion in that national task, between two oceans and between par-
allels situated in regions of ice and tropical seas. They colonized,
they built. They are only at the first stage: it is not sufficiently
realized that the USA is covered with wooden houses. The Capitol in Washington, with many stone columns, is a symbol, a
sign of rooted traditions; the skyscrapers of Manhattan speak of
the spiritual explosion of uncontrolled youth. The Capitol is a
sign of controlled power; the skyscrapers are signs of unchained
power. Power. Middle Ages. One hundred and forty million
individuals whose progenitors all came here in ships, across the
seas, in a pre-medieval invasion. Middle Ages: one hundred and
forty million thinking and acting beings who are equipping themselves, who are examining their souls, who are forging their institutions, their administration, and their thought. A literature is
being born, an art is clearly manifesting itself: first architecture,
classic in its psychological profundity, innovating in everything
which cannot be bound by the irons and chains of tradition.

There is violence, since everything is torn apart—or at least
pulled in two different directions: tradition (having existed)
and the impulse to build everything in a new way.

In short, a battle is raging and no stabilizing treaty is in
sight. One foot is stuck in the thick clay of a past looked upon
as a reassuring truth; the other foot is in the air, looking for a
place and way to set itself down.

There was a pre-medieval period. They were only Barbarians
who came in savage hordes. They were only innumerable hotheads who disembarked in a disorderly way, hotheads because
they had had a faith in God which they wished to preserve; a
faith in a morality which they did not wish to see injured; a taste
for adventure, for a grinding existence wearied them. Hotheads
because they had got into trouble, robbed or killed. Women not
well thought of because they had loved gaiety, etc. . . . Three of
the earth's races, white, black, and yellow, coming to violate the
red race in its own territory: the ensemble of the world. Twenty

peoples, because in reality all these virtues and flaws appear in individuals, whether English, Dutch, Italian, French, Swiss, Spanish, Polish, Russian, Chinese, Japanese, etc. . . .

That invasion was before the Middle Ages. The Middle Ages consist in this: a great people has established itself, has acquired a national unity and, through the minglings and customs imposed by necessity, has created an ethnic unity, a unity of thought, a unity of conscience. This has just come to life in the most recent period of modern times and it opens up a new Middle Age—as in the USSR or in China, as in all of Europe, as in the whole world, a new Middle Age opens up. A civilization has begun. Everything is to be constructed anew: social legislation, institutions, architecture, and thought.

Americans have never ceased to meditate about the moral support of life (an individual event); and they have plunged into a hazardous Puritanism. Today they have set themselves to thinking (a national event); and their inner discipline clashes painfully with the voracity of their gigantic collective enterprise.

There is something dolorous in this tension. In Europe—particularly in France—we have been trained in thinking for a long time. We have humanized the foundations of man's condition. In this matter we are strongest. America is thinking new things and it might someday make a great discovery. The road is long. In the agonies of this struggle in the heart of a new civilization it is necessary to try to see clearly. The anxieties, the timidities, and the brusque, reckless acts natural to youthful forces will be understandable.

SPIRIT OF TRADITION AND FEELING
FOR CONTEMPORARY LIFE

A traditional seriousness is at the bottom of American thought. It is often ridiculed in a disconcerting way. If you think, you are grave. If you do not think, you are like overgrown children, inarticulate cowboys, passionate football players, or passive radio listeners. If you are an important businessman and do not think, you excite yourself with cocktails at five o'clock and are worth nothing afterward; before the cocktails you were a power in Wall Street or in the mid-town skyscrapers—a financial power, with monetary muscles: in that state you buy false Rembrandts.

If students think—when they are not engaged in athletics—they think wisely, gravely, ingenuously, with delight. Thinking is a vocation. With us a streetcar conductor thinks when he is having a good time, at the local bar, with his glass of red or white wine, standing up, expressing personal ideas with a natural simplicity; he always has a word to say, a spontaneous reflection on the passing event; he thinks quickly. We think very quickly and Americans very slowly; we make decisions quickly and Americans very slowly. That is one of the surprising observations that you make in the USA, where time is money. Money is involved in the time taken up by a business transaction, *the time in which things are manufactured.* At that time seconds are as precious as gold. As for us, we undertake nothing, we let the country go to rack and ruin; time has no value. Apéritif time is one of the active moments in French life. On the day that we undertake the construction of new white cathedrals, the thinking capacity acquired around apéritif glasses will produce living works. My lunch at the Plaza and my business dinner in Boston indicate clearly the two qualities of thought, American and French. In spite of all that, throughout the world we succeed in passing as superficial people, as "amusing."

I do not have the time to give to the necessary investigations, nor the taste for plunging into the study of minute facts in order to gain a "scientific" judgment about peoples. I travel with my eyes and ears open, nothing more. I have an experience, acquired by a love of the things of art, which enables me, by that route, to arrive at a revealing judgment. Art is the unconscious, uncontrollable, undefilable expression of an epoch and of the spirit of peoples when they have been sufficiently fashioned by the net woven out of habits, laws, administration, when a unity has been achieved. Art reveals.

There are medieval pictures on the walls of the lounge in my hotel in New York—the Gotham, a middle-class hotel. In my other hotel, the Park Central, there was throughout an ostentatious bazaarlike art. I see quite clearly what the masses are nourished by. We are more developed; more reserved. Alas, completely reserved. We avoid error through abstention. In the secrecy of its laboratories and despite the indifference of the masses, Paris still makes the magnificent art of modern times— a product which France, muzzled by the Academy, does not export, but which foreign countries, enlightened by thinking élites, import.

It was through the Rockefeller Foundation of the Museum of Modern Art in New York that I was invited to go and speak in twenty cities in the USA (the program included forty-two cities but I am not enough of a hero to accomplish such a mission). Notice the two names just mentioned: Museum of Modern Art and Rockefeller Foundation.

Everyone knows that American millionaires, victims of the unlimited piles of gold which they have heaped up in the vicious circle of their own bank accounts, wish to raise up on the ossuary of their fated victims, a socially useful edifice, a work of altruism, thought, instruction, and relief. Carnegie and Rockefeller by themselves have contributed innumerable benefactions. The world is malicious in saying: "Those men need to dissimulate their crimes." You might just as well say: "Those football players do not deceive us by smiling at the photographer after their victory; they have the assassination of their opponents on their consciences." The question is a different one. During the homicidal battles in the Stock Exchange relations between men are not involved, but rather the law of money. Money saved up by economies, gathered together in mountains, engaged in the channels of the infernal machine, takes on a movement which is all its own, it becomes a Niagara, drowns, breaks whatever is in its path, absorbs what is around it with the exactitude and fatality of a physical law, straightens up as a typhoon on the edge of the abyss which it has hollowed out. In order to set up a trophy, money makes hecatombs. Once engaged in the contest, it was normal that Mr. X or Mr. Y should put his passion into winning it; it was necessary to win. To gain here, it was necessary to subtract there. A mechanical, automatic, inhuman, cruel, and indeed a sterile game, since Mr. X or Mr. Y, on top of his mountain of gold, can do no more than sit down to a simple dinner of chicken and spinach—or to put it still more exactly, a bowl of semolina and milk. In this formidable game, in which he was victor, he lost his stomach. He is a simple man like others. He says: If on the one hand I should go on with the ferocious battle of gold, on the other hand, I should like to sow something with my gold through philanthropy. The public insists on talking about a criminal. That is cruel and false. Our millionaire is only a poor man whose name is on the guidepost of the mountain of gold. He remained what he was: normal. Thus Mr. Rockefeller, the founder of the dynasty, imperturbably continued to give ten-cent tips, wherever he was, as in the days when he ate in poor little restaurants. Thus while the grandfather was completely engaged in the ranks of his battling army, his son, Mr. John D. Rockefeller, Jr., and his grandson, Nelson, administered the mountain of gold, but concerned themselves with making it the source of as many social benefits as possible. They have founded the Museum of Modern Art in New York and they take part in guiding it.

I do not know what was in the grandfather's collection; perhaps some Rembrandts, genuine or false. But the Museum of Modern Art in its entirety is given over to better enterprises: revealing to Americans the spirit of the purest researches in the art of today. Landing in New York, I found Fernand Léger in the midst of an exhibition of his work, the best one which had been organized, not forgetting the showing at the Kunsthaus in Zurich. An admirably presented exhibition, without tinsel or extravagance, with an impressive propriety. My architectural exhibition replaced Léger's. Then, immediately afterward, came the Van Gogh exhibition. An attentive public follows these showings. Returning on the *Lafayette*, an optimistic Frenchman said to me: "Your exhibition should have a million visitors." I replied: "Fine, the Van Gogh exhibition, an unprecedented success, had fifty thousand visitors in two weeks.[1] That's terrific! If mine were to have three thousand, I should feel honored. In Paris, sir, Van Gogh would had two thousand and I . . . perhaps thirty-three visitors!"

Following mine, the Museum of Modern Art opened its great exhibition of Cubism and Abstract Art. The catalogue, a magnificent book written by Mr. Barr, the director of the museum, was an up to date summary of the documentation about the advance-guard plastic art of the last forty years; a document which establishes the history—not in intrinsic facts, but through their effects on participants—of the art of this highly revolutionary and creative period.

These are exhibitions, then, of the finest quality. Who visits them? A public of men and women from every vocation, the American élite whose existence you sense in certain attitudes of the skyscrapers, in the bridges, in the colonial style houses, in a section of Fifth Avenue, sometimes in the women's dresses. America is full of a violent desire to learn.

In New York, a hesitating fairy catastrophe, I noted that

1 At the end of the month, one hundred thousand.

French art events have a sparkling purity: Louis Carré's exhibition of African art at Knoedler's, a sumptuous, noble exhibition, a solemn presentation of an art which is above smallnesses; Léger's show, at the Museum of Modern Art; Chirico's show (a perfect selection) at the Pierre Matisse Gallery; that of Jacques Lipschitz (very important and complete) at the Brummer Gallery. They are meteors—the works and the presentation. There is a loving and acute curiosity in American society .

If the French, artists and organizers, bring so much care to the installation in Manhattan of the limpid crystals of contemporary thought, it is because they sense a latent aspiration in the American mass. Real love. The period of false Rembrandts is over.

My first talk in America about the ideas of *Radiant City* took place in the Museum of Modern Art, and the second on the following day in New England, at Hartford, Connecticut. Hartford is a small city which has acquired a reputation through the quality of the undertakings sponsored by its very living museum, the Wadsworth Athenaeum.

It is a museum without great resources, without sensational exhibits. A young museum which has the virtue of presenting works free of all patina: Poussin and Le Nain are clean and full of depth; they seem as if they were painted yesterday. They are cleaned right down to the canvas! It is high time that their example be followed. In this matter also a page is turning; the academic spirit had adjusted itself to the decadence at the end of a civilization: throughout the world works of art were made to lie. The great, courageous artists of all periods were shown to us falsely, under a thick layer of dirt accumulated for centuries. Patina! Distinguished, reassuring, calming, emollient patina, very much in harmony with the dark buildings and the false taste of the interiors. Tintoretto, the variegated colorist, was nothing but a pool of tobacco juice. One day in September 1922—when I was returning home from Venice (Scuola di San Rocco, which shows an ominous abuse of confidence on the part of those charged with the presentation of that treasure! the ceiling black, black, and black, thus they show us Tintoretto's masterpiece)— I visited the museum in Vicenza where a miracle greeted me. A fearless curator had cleaned everything in the museum, completely. The centuries were destroyed; the painting was fresh, as if of yesterday. It was a revelation. The curator told me: "Yes, I scraped everything, took everything off. The works here are *as they were made.*" Now there was strength, where there had been only . . . distinction (what distinction?); a burst of laughter, where one had divined a pale smile; the splendor of colors, where a morass of bitumen had been before. Pictures in color! How incongruous! Enough to send a man—the curator—to the gallows. The fact that Tintoretto was stunning had been completely ignored; no one wished to know that, under Louis XIV, clothing was sparkling, resplendent; that under Louis XV (so distinguished, don't you think?) the hangings, the *toiles de Jouy,* the gilding, the marbles—everything was new and brilliant: a fanfare of colors. . . . Color? It is blood circulating vigorously in the body. Color? It is the very sign of life. The flowers in the gardens and the fields have no patina; the sky is blue in fine weather. The dull accords of plowed earth, of standing rocks, of exposed geological strata, are the solid springboard of those bursts of life which are renewed each spring after the winter: colors!

During 1928, in Moscow, in the atelier for the restoration of icons, I watched the scientific resurrection of Byzantine art. Under a millimeter of successive layers of varnish or repaint, were found works of the eleventh, twelfth, thirteenth, and fourteenth centuries. This art is the direct perpetuation of Greek painting. Brilliance! With friends at Piraeus, in 1933, among the paintings on the prows of coastal sailboats, we discovered the Doric and Ionic orders still strongly flourishing today. Through the centuries painting incarnates diverse moments in time, turned into clean and brilliant colors.

The museum in Hartford, architecturally young, joyously lighted, is worth something because its director, and his friends, have live and hopeful spirits. Springtime can come again to the museums of the world, when the living drive out the academics. Then Poussin and Le Nain will be brought back to life. Suddenly they will be brothers for us today, friends, comrades, co-workers, and no longer the "gentlemen" spoken of in books.

Thus Hartford, a small city in northern Connecticut, has become a spiritual center in America, a place where the lamp of the spirit burns.

The world is perishing from the desire to be "distinguished." Ah! to be able to put your feet in the soup! More politely: not to have always the appearance of a man in a show window, drawn back behind the glass of respectability. What? Do we absolutely have to have marks of distinction, aristocratic particles? Must our remarks always be refined, reserved, and our immense knowledge be just sensed under a careful veil of patina, in a politeness which serves to bluff others? When the cathedrals were white, the stone was raw from the blows of the axe or the chisel, the edges sharp, the features clean, the faces hard. Everything was new, discovery and creation; and stone after stone a civilization was growing. People were happy; they acted. They did not pin labels on each other in honorific Almanachs de Gotha; they did not wear their ranks on sleeves or lapels. There were no Paris salons filled with literary talk; there was no—another embodiment of the same spirit of vanity—Chicago Social Register fixing the number of notable people at four hundred on the basis of the "degree of consideration" in which they are held.

At Hartford I find fifteenth-century Italian tempera panels beside a large, wooden figure of Christ from the Tyrol. No comparison with Praxiteles is possible. I confess that the plaster casts of Praxiteles in the Athens Museum bore me. On the other hand, what a different, true, profound emotion, as spiritual as it is intensely sensual, we feel in the Acropolis Museum, where everything is honest—the period of the so-called "archaic" arts —both the choice and the arrangement of the material. Returning from Athens after the meetings of the International Congresses of Modern Architecture I showed [1] that in the National Museum you could cut through the center with a butter knife and divide the quick from the dead at the precise point at which the Greeks abandoned the short tunic, falling halfway down the thigh, which allowed them to hunt, fight and run, in favor of the toga whose folds flattered the gestures of discourses, hagglings and palavers in the colonnades of the agoras—the exact moment that they began to talk, to "talk well"—which followed the time when they acted. The polychroming of sculpture comes to an end at this time. A crowning epoch, one of supreme distinction? Perhaps. But the top of a curve, if it is the result of an ascent, is destined within itself to be the starting point of the falling line.

Undeterred by the risk of unfavorable criticism, the directors of the Wadsworth Museum organized a series of Negro operas. The Negro question is a thorny one in the USA. The Negroes showed their remarkable abilities in plays, in musical programs, in stage design. It was a "revelation." I shall have something to say about Negro music. But now I am thinking about our "conservatories" (what a significant term!) continuing instruction in the polite way of playing music, when in the USA the Negroes freely express their high spirits and when that immense and splendid body of pure and admirable musical talent is finding itself in relation to and in the face of everything else in the life of the world.

Are these manifestations insignificant at a time of great economic, political, and social crises? They serve to stir up consciousness in a profound way. They introduce new values into the depths of the heart. The horizon changes. The great transformation will come about only through hierarchic elevation. It is through the individual reformation of consciousness that the reformation of collective consciousness will be accomplished.

1 Christian Zervos, "L'Art en Grèce."

When consciousness shall have passed beyond the agonies of its present incertitudes, collective allegiances will develop and a new world will replace a fallen one. That takes time—years are needed, years of sincere self-examination, inner reflection, interior awareness. A collectivity is valuable only through the equilibrium of its material needs. A civilization exists only through the whole immeasurable utterance of an entire society. When individual consciousness has been changed, and only then, the collective mechanism, set right again, will function on a true axis.

The prime movers of the plan for the Hartford Museum do not by any means represent general American aspirations. They appear, rather, like meteors, and as a result, they play a hazardous and exhausting role. The French masses are more ready for self-examination. The American masses form an inert bloc which has its consequence: it is hard to be always thinking about the welfare and the amelioration of the masses when they remain indifferent. The responsibility for fruitful action rests on a few shoulders. Hartford is not something made by the American people; it comes from the presence of individuals of distinction. Such isolation causes certain ravages in the spirits of the élite: the fate of hothouse plants. They are fragile and sensitive and subject to psychological troubles.

My American tour was so filled with days in Pullmans, nights in sleepers, architectural, economic, and city-planning discussions, that it was necessary to forego the dessert proper to those solid repasts: I did not have the time to visit the museums and thus harmonize the food with what is the passion of my life; the consideration of art.

Americans, who are kept very well informed by men who have come to study among us, in Paris, the heart of the laboratory of modern art, or in the provinces of France where the Romanesque churches and cathedrals are, little by little have built up, privately or in public museums, significant collections of modern art. People in Chicago tell you with pride that the treasure of the Art Institute is the *Grande Jatte*, Seurat's most important work. Seurat who died of hunger and disappointment in Paris at thirty-three.

Nevertheless, I saw the remodeled Brooklyn Museum; the director who inaugurated the change, and the curator of prints, explained to me how, in response to government efforts to combat unemployment during the great depression, they had conceived a bold program and carried it through by methods which are worth telling about.

From the outside, the Brooklyn Museum looks like an ineffable academic set-piece; there is a pompous façade surmounted by an army of figures like a row of onions against the sky: muses or demigods, or Revolutionary generals. You enter in a disappointed mood.

Surprise! The surroundings are alive: a vast white space in which circulation is arranged by rationally disposed showcases. The architectural spirit is in control here. For the most part, the collections are made up of "American art," Alaskan totem poles, the painting, jewelry, ceramics, textiles, and architecture of the Incas and Mayas. Great and magnificent art, dominating, exalting the sun and cosmic powers. I am not going to describe it, but simply say how much modern consciousness finds here an eternal vigor. And you also, Museum, through the youthful spirit which animates you the page of black soot has been turned and we are at home.

There were bread lines in the USA. The government granted credits for useful public works. Payments could only be a quarter, a third, a half of normal remuneration. The workers were on the job only a quarter, a third, or a half of a day. Among the unemployed assigned to the remodeling of the museum there were forty architects. There was an obligation to employ them. The director, the workers, and the architects acted as a group. The program was set up after (sometimes) long discussions; the creative spirit, the sense of participation was awakened. After a while they considered the plan their own, to such an extent that,

if an architect made what were thought to be ill-founded criti-
cisms, they did not hesitate to strike.

Such methods would be debatable, if the result were not
there to prove that they succeeded.

EVERYONE AN ATHLETE

The country is covered with universities and colleges for men
and colleges for women. Education is a great concern among
Americans. One of the directors of Princeton University says:
"We make athletes of our young men, including the puny ones."

Everyone an athlete!

The big games in America take place on Saturday afternoon
and bring together in stadiums scattered all over the country
crowds of sixty thousand spectators to watch the two teams. The
big games are played between universities: Yale vs. Princeton,
Columbia vs. Harvard, etc. . . . The study of science and arts
and letters is not compromised. The day has twenty-four hours,
hasn't it—time enough to furnish the spirit and develop the
body?

College? Americans constantly say: "At college . . ." It reflects the presence in their hearts of a great and fine period—the
fine period in their lives. Luxurious fraternities at the universities throughout the country continue to bring together serious
businessmen, and prolong through life the radiance of the years
of youth.

Colleges and universities, then, have a very particular character. Everything in the interest of comfort, everything for the sake of calm and serenity, everything to make solid bodies. Each college or university is an urban unit in itself, a small or large city. But a green city. Lawns, parks, stadiums, cloisters, dining halls, a whole complex of comfortable quarters. Often the style is Gothic—that's the way it is!—rich, luxurious, well made. There is an abundance of money. A millionaire or the widow of a millionaire gladly wills a fortune to the men's or women's college where they were so happy at twenty.

That's fine, I think. Nevertheless, during these splendid visits I think of the life of students in Paris—that of most of them: seventh floor, attic, faucet on the stair landing, Venetian heat in the summer, Siberia in the winter. Dread of solitude in the very center of the immense city. I went through it myself. Is that hard school of life a fruitful education or a public danger? The students of Paris, in poor shape physically, ill fed, living in the promiscuity of alleys and dark stairways, austerely mix the knowledge of the sciences with that of life. It is not in conformity with Taylorism and time for everything. Remaining uncertain, I refrain from passing judgment. In the copious abundance of American colleges bathed in verdure, the poor are fully welcome: there is a perhaps touching method which enables them to enjoy the benefits of college and to achieve their purpose: study, learning. They pay in kind; part of their time is spent in service, in waiting on tables in the dining hall and making up rooms. Americans are eminently democratic; no servitude is involved: I pay my way, hence I am free. Thus, equivalent rights and complete fellowship. Sectarian spirits will declare that the class struggle is involved. Objectively, in the real conditions of the USA, this seemed to me an intelligent and generous solution.

The American university is a world in itself, a temporary paradise, a gracious stage of life.

. . . I make a trip to Vassar, a college for girls from well-to-do families. From New York the car plunges north into Westchester; when the slums of New York have been left behind, you enter a Parkway, a recent American development which consists of automobile highways carried through attractive sites: the pavement, framed by borders, is perfect; intersections are at different levels. Everything that could have occasioned purely technical and perhaps strongly architectural solutions is, on the contrary, dominated by a landscapist's thought. Pretexts are sought to pass over intersecting roads on picturesque bridges; curved junctions wind among rocks, fine shrubs, flowers, and lawns. Parkways will cover the whole extent of the USA with a sinuous, charming, picturesque—and slightly arranged—network of roads. Louis XIV or Napoleonic epics, of which there are notable examples in France: those straight routes indifferent to hills and valleys, seemingly made for driving, along which cars move gaily, are replaced by delicately arranged layouts. It is something quite different; I should deplore the replacing of one by the other. It is better that both exist, answering different purposes: the pastoral and the heroic.

There is a radio in the Ford. Not an unsatisfactory one, a good radio; that is a national virtue. It is an autumn afternoon, Indian summer. The surprisingly dark red leaves are gone. We hear a piano fragment: "Theme and Variations" by Aaron Copland. Then piano and chorus. In the intellectual vacancy of this excursion at sixty miles an hour, the music caught on the wing has an attractive charm. American music. Here also a new development is taking shape.

We arrive at the college "within a budding grove."

The buildings are scattered over lawns in a splendid park. Before my speech, I go to see the theater where I am to talk. A dozen girls are taking down the sets of a play put on the evening before. They designed and executed the sets themselves: framework, plywood panels, saws, nails, hammers, and pliers, jars of color and brushes. They are in overalls or in bathing suits. I enjoy looking at these beautiful bodies, made healthy and trim by physical training.

The buildings have the atmosphere of luxurious clubs. The girls are in a convent for four years. A joyous convent.

Two hours later the theater is invaded by six hundred of them. "Good heavens," I say to myself, fortified by previous experiences at American universities, "how am I going to hold the attention of those twelve hundred laughing eyes?" I talked in French throughout my tour. Make a sounding, try a facetious remark. It works! They got it, everyone understood! I never had a more responsive audience during my trip. It is a pleasure and I amuse myself by developing the bold theses for which these women will be the best propagandists. After the lecture there is a mob scene: they rush onto the platform and seize five or six large drawings I have just done. To put on walls of the dining room or study? Not at all! They rip them apart, tear them up, cut them into small pieces. A piece for each Amazon. Pens in hand, they cry: "Sign, sign!"

When the circumstances are favorable—and they were at Vassar—I take great pleasure in making large, ten-foot, colored frescoes which become the striking stenographic means, enlivened by red, green, brown, yellow, black, or blue, for expressing my *Radiant City* theses or my ideas about the reorganization of daily life: architecture and city planning, bearers of the "essential joys" of machine age civilization. Thus, in the USA, I did three hundred yards of these drawings (six rolls of paper fifty yards in length); they are somewhere in the homes of listeners, or in the universities. I improvise, each time I attack the problem from a different angle; I am pleased by the difficulty involved in getting the forms within the limits of the paper. The drawings at Vassar had a particular verve. The Amazons reduced them to confetti!

At the buffet they did almost as much for me. Some asked my companion whether I preferred blondes or brunettes, others nearly annihilated me with the weight of their questions. I am dumfounded by the nature of the questions: sociology, economics, psychology. They are well informed about the serious problems of our days. They speak impeccable French. During their college course they may spend a year in France. I have never felt so stupid: "But I am ignorant of the problems which concern you; I am only a city planner and an architect and perhaps an artist. You overwhelm me, you are too serious, I must be excused, I am going to join the people who are eating cookies!"

There are twelve hundred girls at Vassar.

Curfew is sounded. Some of us meet for a glass of whiskey at the home of a woman who teaches art history. She says that the Ecole des Beaux-Arts in Paris has caused much trouble. A brilliant student who is present is devoting herself to a study of Caravaggio. "You women are also interested in Caravaggio? Why Caravaggio? Because of the psychological turmoil in that equivocal personality. Do you also feel a kind of frustration?" One of the men who teaches the history of art is likewise a student of Caravaggio! Caravaggio, rising from the past, nourishes a part of the American spirit; further, contemporary surrealism has won over the USA, the USA of the hesitant and the troubled.

At Vassar College you discover the hard problems of the American economy, and the uncertainty in the spirit of the American élite. These twelve hundred girls, constantly renewed, are preparing themselves for a great task. In the society of the USA women play a part through their intellectual efforts.

Many of the girls are on the Saturday morning train taking me back to New York. They come to the single smoking car to have a cigarette among big, solid dock workers and men employed in factories along the Hudson River. Democratic spirit. In the luxurious setting of Vassar I noticed some communistic sympathies. It is a regular experience: the good society intelligentsia, well to do and liberal spenders, are prepared for the great overturning with a touching ingenuousness.

The train follows the very wide river. I note that, for crossing these broad expanses of water, America has only one type of bridge, the suspension bridge, the bridge of modern times, straight and filigreed, without regard for the traditional means of architectural poetry. Full of poetry of its own.

Princeton University, a men's college, is located symmetrically south of New York. An immense institution, a university city composed of parks as far as you can see. At the moment, Princeton is leading the American soccer league. That is not an insignificant fact! Holding the cup or fighting to win it is an intense springboard of solidarity and enthusiasm.

I am faced with the same question: is it a good thing for students to pass four years of happiness in a paradise; or is it better in their student days that they know the whole face of life, with its flaws, its misery, its anguish, its greatness?

These solid boys—all of them athletic—this material security, this simple joy in fellowship, this effortless existence of the young members of the tribe sheltered from contrary winds, this all-pervasive cleanliness, this exceptional domestic comfort, such are the opportunities on the credit side of the American ledger. With us the balance-sheet column is empty. On both sides, I grant that the opportunities for learning, and the manner, are in balance and they are one of the magnificent conquests of civilization.

With us there is no chance of being athletes at the end of our studies!

Throughout the USA the tribes of students camp in luxury. They have their own regulations, their own independent administration, they have the right to initiate programs, they have duties associated with sport. Someone has written that American students have good, frank heads and the eyes of calves. American students live in flocks in rich pastures; French students seem to live individually or in those small groups that form friendships; there are no rich pastures here, but only the atmosphere of lecture rooms in the midst of the arid city. I keep turning the question over, the problem I turn around. I am attracted by the pathos of life and danger; much less by the assurance of spoiled papa's boys, well fed, well washed, well buttoned up. I say to myself: they are deprived of a powerful food: difficulty. If I add up the operations involved and line them up one after another, I see quite plainly that studying is studying (nose in the books, serene mind, well-furnished stomach, warm room). And that, perhaps, there is a time for everything. When you plant beans it is not customary to put paving stones over them to keep them from growing straight.

American universities are large, rich tribes encamped in the midst of greenery, with the detachment from events which the widespread Gothic style brings. It expresses rather well a type of ideal life, Elysian, theoretical, Paradise to begin life, Hell afterward; a provisional Garden of Eden in which there would be happiness if the boys and girls did not have their own spiritual uncertainties, like everyone else. Nothing more is needed to restore man to his torment and anxiety.

At Princeton I made two talks about architecture and city planning and I conducted a seminar or conference with students in the form of a criticism of the plans for a villa. Architecture is taught there by an intelligent and liberal-spirited Frenchman. And yet at Princeton, as at Columbia, as at Yale, as at the Massachusetts Institute of Technology, and everywhere else, the spirit of the new times does not blow with the strength of a gale. One thing explains another. If the skyscrapers of Manhattan and Chicago are, in their very essence, a paradox, it is because the intellectual gymnastics which make minds supple in the period of professional training, do not exist. American instruction is very . . . American, I mean timid, full of reservations, timorously founded on Vignolesque traditions. For years, graduates of universities on every continent have come to my atelier in Paris. Without being able to come to a conclusion, I try to formulate a judgment about the various kinds of instruction in France, Germany, Italy, Spain, England, the USA, Switzerland, Czechoslovakia, Yugoslavia, the USRR, Holland, Belgium, Poland, Scandinavia, Uruguay, Greece, etc. . . . Academism has sent down roots everywhere. The teachers, usually retired from the practice of the craft of architecture, avoid risking themselves in adventures. They would not incur such a risk unless they were driven to it by the hammer blows of creative passion, of participation, of controversy. Yet if the teacher builds, no one expects bold initiatives from him: he is of the School, his work will be of "the School"; security for the client. Nevertheless, the Dutch are relatively free of bias. The Czechs believe in "modern" and the Polish also. The Uruguayans are going forward even though two steps away, in Buenos Aires, until recently, they were locked in the strong-box security of the styles. Switzerland and Czechoslovakia produce serious technicians; the Czechs are subtle, the Swiss heavier. The Czechs draw with remarkable acuteness and finesse. From Germany came young people "liberated" by the Bauhaus, the school founded by Walter Gropius and closed by Hitler; they were inclined to be aesthetes; they quickly considered themselves "artists," and they lacked the serious foundation of the English, the Swiss, the Czechs, and the Poles. The virtue of the plan, the elegance of the solution, eminently French values, are unknown everywhere else. Such a lack of spirituality saddens me. The practical spirit dominates. The Ecole des Beaux-Arts in Paris would emerge victorious if its aims were other than constantly striking effects reached by graphical methods which infallibly lead to Orsay stations or Grands-Palais. I give my full confidence to the students and wish them to enjoy some breaths of air—a typhoon! Current architecture is sad, caged, chlorotic, nerveless, spiritless, without consciousness of its means. The School kills, the schools kill, by being shut off far from crafts and materials. Reality is lacking. Schools end their training with diplomas, soporifics, when they should end with a stiff kick in the pants which would force young people to jump into the water, to open their eyes and minds and to undertake their own spiritual creation. Alas! I have a penchant for wishing to make supermen, while administrations have created diplomas in order to sanctify themselves, first by legitimizing their own existence and then for the sake of spreading security through the country.

Security first! So much the worse if individuals waste away, society will have its reassuring architecture! The harvest is finally ripe wherever this lethargy, distilled in the schools in all countries, has borne fruit: architecture has been killed! The instruction is a sequestration of youth in the mold of the past; not the opening up of the immense, attractive unknown of tomorrow.

In the instruction at American universities I think I observe a sort of fear of seeing the doors open on the unknown of tomorrow. The students are serious, balanced, calm; they acquire grades and general coverage insurance. In the halls of M.I.T. I saw huge machines hung on the walls, wash drawings, representing palaces or mausoleums. Boring, shameful. Surrounded by students and some of their teachers, I said: "How is it that you have not done away with these horrors?"

When I speak in the architectural lecture rooms of universities in the USA, I have the feeling that I am presenting dangerously disturbing ideas. They listen to me in a silence that makes me feel that I am not being understood. I throw myself into my large drawings; I put in red, blue, green, black; I write comments, figures. I conclude in a still petrified atmosphere. A student from Columbia came to my hotel to talk to me: "Your one-hour lecture was worth as much to us as three years of our regular course."—"Really?"—"Yes, and we are unanimous about it." How locked up these young people are!

In my seminar at Princeton I am discussing the plans for a villa. In them there are many charming spots designed as successive delights. I say: "It is necessary to choose and limit, to condense: of these scattered good designs, you must make the good design, the true one, the right one!" Expressing myself (modestly!) in the manner of Montaigne, I conclude: "Gentlemen, you never have more than one bottom to sit down on!" The teacher and the chairman of the department are present. Silence and embarrassment.—"Will you translate that, please?" —No, you will not translate such a remark in the beautiful, green, Gothic town of Princeton.

In the white corridor leading to the lecture hall there are three pictures: a Matisse, a Rouault, a Derain. It is only a temporary exhibition, other pictures will take their place—sometimes a single picture. They circulate among various universities and come from private collections. A typewritten explanatory note is pinned up beside each picture. It is an excellent thing, refreshing, cheering. From the start I have said: the USA is full of good will.

I am perfectly conscious of course that, in the nature of things, colleges and universities—in a word, education—are at once the seat of the conquests of the spirit, and simultaneously, a break in them. A schoolmaster escapes from life. He is a functionary with characteristic reflexes and eccentricities. You can understand, then, this cry from the heart spoken by the wife of my first drawing teacher: a new, socialist municipal government had retired him after forty-five years of teaching; he was overwhelmed, upset in his daily habits.—"Those swine could have left him at his post until his death!"

Thus, education will always be torn between two fatalities: apostleship and egoism. The organization of the schools should result in the checking of one and the stimulation of the other. By the law of contrasts the USA should be open to apostleship and free to break it in a brutal way if, at some time, it should run counter to the ferocious demands of economic battles. Wilson knew something about that.

In the Middle West, not far from Detroit (the fief of Ford) Cranbrook Academy is a fitting corollary of the violent life of the USA.

About 1900 there was a talented young architect at Helsingfors in Finland: Eliel Saarinen. He was known to the architectural world through various works and, about 1922, he took part in the Chicago Tribune Tower competition. His design was passed by. But an important industrialist noticed it, recognized in it the qualities of a genuine sensibility. In the country of the timid people, sensibility sometimes takes on the violence of a volcano. The industrialist asked Saarinen to come to America; he offered him a magnificent piece of ground out in the country. "Build what you consider useful for the development of American sensibility." Thus Cranbrook Academy was born. It is a retreat; a place where young men and young women come to study art, plunging into an atmosphere of beatification in the midst of fields and woods. They philosophize at work, they philosophize at meals; masters and students all eat together.

It is all a little farfetched, somewhat cut off from life. A result of the harshness of American life. An outpouring of self, a convent, a monkery: "My son, pray for my salvation, for one who is obliged to engage in the hard battle of money! . . ."

The buildings were designed by Saarinen. Thus, in Germany, at Hellerau near Dresden, was born a mystic town about 1910. A spiritual center, or one that wished to be so. If society is hostile to meditations it recognizes the usefulness of "monkeries." They can be as extravasated from the whole of life as the brutal life of business is deprived of true life. Thus, wisdom is lacking. Cranbrook, a paradisaic retreat for disheartened combatants, is very American.

The American professor is as different as possible from the businessman. Business pushes back the years of college into a radiant mirage. Today, the violence of Manhattan or Chicago, of Detroit or Pittsburgh, etc. Yesterday, heads bent over studies, "while there is still time." Around youth, dedicated or undedicated teachers. Quietude of university centers. Caste of teachers somewhat weakened by such a beautiful retreat in the midst of restricted Capuan delights. I like Manhattan and Chicago. Nevertheless, I am convinced that teachers have a role of capital importance, provided that the sap of the real flows from time to time through the verdant cities of study. When I had finished my talk about the ideas of the *Radiant City* at Cranbrook, the founder and Maecenas came up to shake my hand and said sadly: "But art, sir, what do you do about art?" The new times will discover the law of tomorrow in the furnace of cities. And art is not hatched in incubators.

CARAVAGGIO AND SURREALISM

Let's return to the Vassar girl absorbed in the study of Caravaggio.

Caravaggio, an Italian painter of the sixteenth century, "worked in a studio which was painted black; light came in only through a small overhead opening." Stop! Through him we discover a corner of the American soul. If we connect Caravaggio with contemporary surrealism, which is well represented in American collections, our diagnosis will be confirmed. This chapter draws us into the tangled catacombs of consciousness frequented by troubled, youthful hearts.

Caravaggio in university studies, surrealism in collections and museums, the inferiority complex which obsesses those who wish to break away from the simple arithmetic of numbers, the principle of family disturbances, the funereal spirit which appears in the hours of spiritual creation—that is the unexpected harvest which overloads my arms at the end of my first trip to the USA, in which I was concerned with the study of questions of city planning. Enough material to write a book in which these unexpected conclusions would be supported by arguments and sufficient proofs. City planning, which is bound up with the essential elements in the profound actions of a society, opens up indiscreet windows.

This inadvertently lifted veil which discloses devotions to Caravaggio, an Italian painter with a very disquieting mentality, a very talented painter, well thought of in the intellectuual circles of the USA, reveals, under well-bred external appearances, a complex disturbance and the anxieties of sexual life. Something is taking place in the very heart of being. Having observed that, my mind takes hold of a series of small manifestations as far removed as possible from the grandeur of the skyscrapers.

And the grandeur of the skyscrapers is suddenly explained. I realize that I am in the country of the timid people.

In its gigantomachy American city planning betrays a timidity which is a hazard at the very moment when it would be desirable to react and act rightly; it is the result of a lack of equilibrium, of unbalance, and it carries with it rather serious disturbances of the core of the social cell—the key of everything: the family.

I am afraid that I shall not be pardoned for being so indiscreet.

When a society has acquired its equilibrium, its maturity, its gestures and actions are clear, healthy, normal. The fundamental law of nature, the perpetuation of the species, no longer involves religious ritual, or uneasy hesitations, or violence, or fear. An action which has become conscious, it has moved to the plane of art. It is ennobled by the contribution of the imagination, aesthetic feeling, the cult of the beautiful. The idea of "art" implies knowledge, consciousness, mastery, perpetual discovery within the modest framework of available values, the mathematics of an ingenious, fertile, and infinitely varied equation. Art is above all constructive, positive, creative. A door opening on the unknown, discoverer of the new, maker of the new, maker of life. And not a collection of souvenirs, a museum of souvenirs, a memorial of souvenirs, an accumulation of dead things, even rare or sublime ones. The perpetuation of the species is a cosmic law; love, human creation, in the luminous joining together of sensuality and aesthetics. Both dominate societies in a varying degree, according as uneasiness or mastery is in control.

Today, then, a page of human history turns; all life opens up to be grasped in armfuls. An art has to be created entirely anew, made up of new relations, a stairway which rises up before us, regularly, in solid, successive, and reassuring steps.

The stairway already climbed, which falls away behind us, which the enlightenment of the spirit and natural causes have superseded, throwing it into shadow and even darkness? Those are singularly disturbed spirits who wish to climb it again, descend it once more, and consequently, to renounce what is before us! Spirits upset by fear, apprehension, anxiety, anguish—frustration.

Caravaggio had his studio painted black; a sepulchral light fell from a small opening. His case belongs to psychiatrists. Is it in the name of art, Vassar student, that you enter that sewer? I believe that you were impelled by an unsatisfied heart.

European surrealism, born in the uncertainty of war, triumphed in the unchained postwar period. It opposed itself to cubism, the lucid gesture of constructive spirits seeking the conquest of the new times. Cubism is a powerful revolution. The discernment of new times. Health, strength, optimism, creation, the contribution of a few strong and healthy men. Someday it will be recognized that cubism was one of the decisive hours of the general revolution. Surrealism is a noble, elegant, artistic, funereal institution.

It was necessary to embalm and hide under flowers the remains of a dead society; chants and prayers were required. The altar is prepared and there are trophies on it. There are the green flames of a ceremony in memory of so many things that were. Purple curtains lighted by green flames, the evocation of ghosts, desubstantialization, dematerialization. Dream! Freud! Phantoms in limbo! Almost spiritism. Spiritualism, stories, evocation. Literature. There are no bones in it any longer, but disjointed things, unearthly, passing over into stupefying and promiscuous combinations. Sensitive souls, lacking in solidity, occupy themselves with these precious, crepuscular decorations. The sea withdraws; at the horizon the sun bleeds upon the exceedingly green water; there are ruins in the form of a cenotaph, the clouds are in tatters; fragments of columns lie on the ground; by association, cut up torsos of women and dark blood, birds, a horse of the decadent period of antiquity. Symbols, abbreviations, evocations. What liturgy is this? What refined, moving, spectral ceremony? What appeal to the past? Is it an entombment? They are burying what was, what has ceased to be. They are weeping over the dead. It is an excellent thing.

That is understood! But the ceremony is reaching its end. The new world is waiting for workers!

The intelligentsia of the USA gives its attention to these funeral rites. This country, which as yet is familiar only with technical maturity, faces the future uneasily. The American soul seeks refuge in the bosom of things that were. That is the present stage.

The people in the USA who concern themselves with art (art historians, professors, directors of museums) are exceptional persons; their refined sensibility, their complete sincerity, their love, find standing around them the skyscrapers of Wall Street, the great bridges of New York, the stockyards of Chicago, Ford and his rationalized production, Pittsburgh and its blast furnaces. What a wall of stone, what a wall of fire, what an armature of steel! Advertising, the almighty dollar, time is money, the hundred-page newspaper, what crushing and suffocating forces! Day after day they are increasingly isolated, but also stronger. The body of the USA—which I have often drawn: enormous hands, titanic shoulders, feet like bridge foundations—appalls them. Nevertheless, all his energies given over to the hard labor of each day, the giant commands that thought and art live.—"What I do (for you see that I am caught in the gears—I struggle, I defend myself, I win), son, is not necessary for you. You who are free, prepare him, after my hard crossing through the Alps, for the imminent delights of Capua. . . ."

The blinding light of the blast furnaces of Pittsburgh and the yellow brilliance of gold are the accomplices of the green flames in the crypt of Caravaggio and on the altars of surrealism, bleeding with sacrifices and roses.

"QUAT'Z' ARTS" IN NEW YORK

"The men are tired of everything, the women are tired of the men"—remark made by an editor of one of the smartest fashionable magazines in America during the Quat'z' Arts Ball in New York.

"The women live with themselves; the men are in the city; the women seek entertainers or amuse themselves in the company of other women. American women are dominators and they dominate." (If you envisage a certain kind of society, you can get to the bottom of the import of these remarks.) A confidence expressed by a woman of the best society in a very handsome salon—the American style made up of Italian Renaissance and modern things molded together by the liveliest kind of feeling for contemporary life.

It should be clear, of course, that there is no question here of the great mass of the American people, but rather of the society which is formed by the tumult of capitals, places of enrichment, which, in all countries, is the barometer of significant currents. Persons useful to study because the fever that devours them reveals fundamental causes.

These two avowals have a negative character. The cultivated American, once he is pulled away from his business affairs, talks freely about his inferiority complex. Each time I am embarrassed by that gesture of humility; I see an erect Manhattan, the drives of Chicago, Ford in Detroit, and so many clear signs of youthful power. They seem to see a flash of steel in our glance and, behind our foreheads, a well-oiled chain of tests, appraisals, judgments. Certainly we reflect, we weigh, we try to see where things are going. Confronted by our considered approval, the pre-Hitler Germans often said: "You think that we are Barbarians, don't you?"

The Quat'z' Arts Ball is to be held in the immense rooms of the Waldorf-Astoria in New York. I shall go. First there is a visit to the costume company. The theme of the ball is: An *Exotic Festival in India*. I have always been suspicious of these imaginative courts. You fall from a height, you return to reality, you see what people are: what they wish to seem. In Montparnasse it is different, the artists are free (the good ones). At the gala celebrations on steamships or at costume balls on land, the goddess "Creation" is rather small and king "Pride" is fully inflated.

Quat'z' Arts in New York? Something to intrigue a Parisian. We shall see exhibitions by former students in painting and architecture at the Beaux-Arts in Paris. But in reality, aside from the effects of alcohol and the frankly nudist tendency of the Quat'z' Arts in Paris, on this absurd occasion the spirit has never shown itself like a phenomenon of spontaneous generation, has it? Alas, no, and again no! As the painting is, so are the architecture, the decoration, the ball. The little nude women brighten the affair, of course, and that is what makes it go.

At the Waldorf-Astoria there will be no little nude women, oh never!

The costume man wants to rig me out with a turban and a brocaded robe; this evening, for the same amount of money, I can be a rajah or a khan.

No usurped title, thank you! Not being a handsome fellow, I keep my anatomy out of sight. In spite of some protests, I insist on white and blue striped convict's trousers and an Indian army guard's vermilion coat (he would have loved to see me in a high-ranking officer's coat!); I find an enormous gold epaulette which I fasten on the left side. No military cap, sir, a white, pointed clown's hat, please. For color balance I put on a dark blue sash as a shoulder-belt, cut by a gold band. There are no pockets in my convict's trousers: bills go into my socks, my pipe and tobacco pouch into my belt. To finish off, three differently shaped spots of white on my cheeks and forehead, to perplex the curious.

If everyone does likewise, there will perhaps be some amusing sights!

It was a tremendous ball; three thousand costumed dancers. There were elephants, bears, clowns, and acrobats. Everyone was bedecked, covered with brocades, with plume turbans, Indian scarfs, shimmering silk; the ensemble was lusterless and flat, dull and without the least brilliance. Brilliance does not require silk. To achieve effects of color in costume many neutral tones are needed, and judicious accents of color, and mat stuffs. The Russian ballets of Diaghilev, "Parade," "The Three-Cornered Hat," designed by Picasso, taught us that. When the elephants came in there was a really sumptuous effect. In a particolored crowd, dressed up in silk, the gray skin of an elephant becomes a luxurious costume.

Everyone was handsome, and how! Clean-shaven, powdered, respectable, solemn. Everyone wisely displayed notable honors, all those of the East and Far East, from the emir to the rajah to the mandarin. Beggars? There are no people in rags at the festival in the midst of the skyscrapers! When you are a maharajah or governor of the English East Indies, you have to parade your costume. How many nobles there were that evening! Once a year masked balls help to satisfy the ambitions which struggle against the realities of everyday life. The light music does not succeed in shaking off the collective stiffness. As for me, my fate was soon settled. I was a discordant note; I was neither mad nor clownish, I was a sore thumb. I was out of place. I did not arouse the slightest smile, the slightest astonishment, the slightest curiosity, the slightest interest. Lost, poor fellow, I was the only one of my type, disagreeable, disapproved, rejected. I left ingloriously, thrust aside by respectability.

Conversation continued to be serious. A gentleman dressed like a Shakespearean ambassador said to me: "The 'civilization of the west' [poor France] is finished. In the USA and in Europe it's all over, we shall never accomplish anything again; there are others surging up in the East!" I am willing to admit that the East, India or China, will speak to us in a useful way at some time, in a profound way. It will speak to us of ethics and not of dumping. I reply: "With its two thousand years, France is not old, the USA is young and has just begun!"

With three spots on my face, I feel that my friends should laugh at me for being concerned with such serious thoughts. But not at all! At the masked ball, the ambassador in purple, the mandarin in green, the maharajah with a plume discuss with me unfathomable problems.

THE FAMILY DIVIDED

I am risking a dangerous hypothesis. It is not with impunity that, in its first century, machine age society inconsiderately constructed its cities against the grain. The city-dwelling place, shelter of the family, of work and pleasure, accompanies the life of men, step by step. If the city is false, wrong, against common sense, the life of men is affected by it; and, denaturalized by the milieu which they have made for themselves, they undergo dangerous avatars. *The twentieth century has not built for men; it has built for money!* (Remark from my book, *The Radiant City,* later printed as an exergue in the reform program of the Union of War Veterans, of which 800,000 copies were published in France.) How do you measure that? By the fundamental social element, by the cell of the social body, by the family. In the USA the family is disturbed. I noted the admissions of that a moment ago. For a long time I have looked for the damage done to life by the gigantic machinery of the disordered city: the distended cities of our times. In the USA the diagnosis comes out better than elsewhere, since they have worked on a larger scale, pushed the phenomenon to its limits.

Urban zones are no longer cities, but regions. In the case of Chicago and New York their diameter is more than sixty miles. They saw the problem in a large way? No, they saw it in a false way. The sun establishes a twenty-four-hour day. Its course is too rapid to allow the accomplishment of the essential functions of life in their daily cycle. They wished to dominate the situation, to stop up the crack through which equilibrium flows away: they used speed. The sun goes even faster. They constructed Pullmans, subways, highways, roads, and covered the country with swarms of automobiles. The country is on wheels; everything rolls. You are free because you are on the road at the wheel of your own car, because you can read the paper in the train! Industry is kept busy in creating this gigantic mass of machinery. I think that it is an illness. I said: "Yes, the cancer is in good health." My second series of talks could not get away from the same obsession; I spoke of the Great Waste and I saw that you had forged chains for yourselves. At the end of the series, I discover that the fundamental social element is ill: the family is cut in two.

The great waste can be analyzed. I shall do that later. It leads to hard labor. Life becomes nothing more than a battle without hope of victory. Day after day, an unbalanced situation. The atmosphere of the city is exciting, intoxicating, but exhausting. Half of this intense effort serves no useful purpose, simply makes wind. In the evening, you very much need to get away from it all. I have mentioned the cocktail parties at five o'clock, with fifty people standing up in a single room. You get up early in the morning and, in your car (a wonderful domestic tool, inexpensive and easily kept up—for mass production has made possible the organization of maintenance, repair, exchange), you

arrive at the station of that distant, verdant suburb. You catch
the train. Often you have breakfast on it. You read the paper. In
New York, you take a bus or subway—preferably the subway,
which is the only thing that travels quickly, since the streets are
completely, totally ill. You ascend to your skyscraper office.
There, it's advertising and competition—a battle. You have lunch
with other men at the counter of a restaurant in the skyscraper;
the equipment is perfect, the service rapid. You quickly start to
work again. After a cocktail, subway, bus, train, and evening
paper. Your car is lined up with a hundred others at the station;
it has been waiting quietly since morning. You drive away and
arrive at home. You see your wife again at eight o'clock in the
evening.—"Hello, hello. . . ." Well, she has been alone for twelve
hours of the day. She has her life also, but with a quite different
kind of time. She has seen her friends, she has read books, she
has gone to lectures, to exhibitions; her mind is furnished with
things different from those that have been going around in her
husband's head—which continue to go around. The husband is
a little uncomfortable. How to pick up the thread? How are such
different voltages to go together in unity? They are not in harmony. In the USA women are inclined to take an interest in
the things of the spirit. Her life, which she organizes by herself,
is expensive. A lot of money is needed. The economy of the
USA, devoted to waste, pours out torrents of dollars, but you
can't put many of them in your pocket. Seven hours of the day
serve no useful purpose: four spent in sterile business activity
and three in transportation. I have the feeling that in general
these men and women, in spite of all their good will, have difficulty in communicating with each other. So it is every day
throughout life. As a result the husband is intimidated, thwarted.
The wife dominates. A great need of something other than business fills men's hearts, and contact is impossible because the
voltages are different. Every day there is a kind of distance between them, a kind of trench. There are demands, the woman
makes a kind of claim. For the man, the woman is like a dream

difficult to take hold of. He showers her with attentions—money, jewels, furnishings, comfort, luxury, vacations. He is in a sort of perpetual arrears. The man works for the sake of arriving some day. Arriving where? He will be too late. Worn out.

Others have observed the same thing. I think I have discovered the cause; I risk this hypothesis: the family is divided because the cities are built against all common sense. Thus the "great waste" is paid for in a cruel way.

Jokingly they say: "In the United States men die at fifty because of the hard lives their wives lead them."

FUNEREAL SPIRIT

"Funereal entrances of the Empire State Building (the largest skyscraper, which has since been dethroned by Rockefeller Center). . . . The black of polished stones, the walls faced with dark, gleaming slabs. . . . And, in the show windows of Fifth Avenue dress shops, those dominating wax manikins: Aeschylus!"

After that in my notebook there is a phrase which is a cry of despair: "There are no trees in the city! . . . The tragic quality of a violent life which is distended, torn between the pole of powerful action and the other pole (which is the issue at the bottom of each heart: 'All the same, I am a man . . .')."

"Hello, old man!" A jovial slap on the back.

A cordially outstretched hand: "How are you?"

A cordiality which still implies the immense extent of the

country and the joy of meeting and the pleasure in doing a service.

How fundamentally sympathetic! A friendly hand, an open smile, and a heart of gold.

But God knows that gold is a crusher of hearts.

This power has sprung up almost spontaneously, through the machine, space, colonization. And the experience of being one of the greatest voices of the world has come too suddenly. Awakening of the feeling of responsibility. A charge on conscience. Having unconsciously initiated a civilization. Suddenly seeing it rise up in twenty years in the sky of Manhattan, its arms in the air, a phenomenon beyond imagination, not a harmonious phenomenon, a spontaneous generation—an explosion! To be suddenly obliged to play a great role. To find oneself at the moment of variation of the curve in which resolute action implies the spiritual conclusion. To pass from instinctive devices to the clear-sighted gesture of thought.

Here, in the fact which is *today*, in the United States, a great voice of modern times, the nature of this event is so unexpected, the leap is so high, that breath may be lacking. It is a serious hour. In a moving, gathering together of its forces, the United States measures its responsibility and becomes grave. Anguish. Smiles do not play around the hearts of young men; anxiety digs itself in. Smiles are part of the enterprises of mature men, because they know: they have tried, experimented, judged, decided, chosen. Smiles belong to maturity.

Before this feeling of responsibility to the world developed, the USA went to Florence or to the cathedrals of France to look for the means of satisfying its taste for grace and its inclination toward daring. The USA still went to school to others. In the matter of important architecture, they did what they had done so well for two centuries in domestic building: made a truly creative adaptation of other people's ideas—skyscrapers, "Renaissance" apartment houses, and "colonial style" homes. About 1925, through a profound inner impulse, they realized that the new times were here and that it was necessary to express them in architecture. The skyscrapers of Manhattan became "modern." After that the work "of others" no longer counted. It was necessary to create. I repeat: they were serious and solemn, as young people are. Money was plentiful; solemnity had unlimited credit. Unusual, gigantic dimensions, luxurious materials drove the continent that used them toward its true expression: stiffness; dignity affected by melancholy; richness which is not yet the product of elegant, supple, complex mathematics—of proportion—but that of exaggerated dimensions and the heaping up of opulent materials.

Here is the measure of spirit: through products, programs, or materials, it creates something "rose" or it creates something "black." In the entrances of skyscrapers, in the halls of skyscrapers, in the lobbies of moving-picture palaces and theaters, a funereal spirit reigns, a solemnity which has not yet succeeded in coming alive.

Outside, in the street, along Broadway, on the other hand, the night streams with mobile lights. Inside, the burlesque shows, movies, revues, are never joyous, but rather tragic or desperately sentimental. To shake the people out of their seriousness, Hollywood has invented some astonishing types, Charlie Chaplin, the imperturbable ordinary man, Buster Keaton, tragically isolated in his individual activity, Laurel and Hardy, indifferent to circumstances. These comic movies touch the bottom of the American soul, they show what is true: a man concerned with the simple problems of his own heart finds himself, from the very fact of that legitimate preoccupation, swimming against a disproportionately swollen current. The simple man is imperturbable, a good fellow full of friendly and altruistic thoughts which are often puerile. Around him, an overwhelming situation, inhuman dimensions. That disproportion is the rule in the USA: an abyss opens up before sensitive persons at every step. In reality, it is less amusing than in the movies. It is a serious matter, pathetic, upsetting.

I went to the Automobile Show. There can be no argument about American machinery. It is up to the minute. But the cars are heavy and overstuffed. That is the kind of feeling you get from them. The spectacle of the streets is made oppressive by them.

The funereal spirit exists in what is called "the architecture of things."

THE SPIRIT OF THE MACHINE, AND NEGROES IN THE USA

Here again there is an abyss between delicate hearts and the atmosphere of frenzy. Negro music has touched America because it is the melody of the soul joined with the rhythm of the machine. It is in two-part time: tears in the heart; movement of legs, torso, arms and head. The music of an era of construction: innovating. It floods the body and heart; it floods the USA and it floods the world. Hence, everything in our auditory habits changes. Psycho-physiologically it is so powerful, so irresistible that it has torn us from the passivity of listening and has made us dance or gesticulate, participate. It has opened the cycle of sound of modern times, turned the page on the conservatories. New cadences, new cries, unknown groups of sounds, an exuberance, a flood, a vertiginous intensity. . . . Launched by the Negroes, it is American music, containing the past and the present, Africa and pre-machine age Europe and contemporary America. Taught on the plantations of Louisiana, the Negroes learned hymns and folk songs. Folklore of the best quality: Gregorian chants, Dutch-English psalms, German and Tyrolean lieder, etc. They swayed their heads and swung their arms and legs as they repeated them. In them the depths of equatorial Africa rise again. But they live, crowded together, in Harlem or Chicago, in slums near the skyscrapers. They serve in Pullmans, in coaches, in all-night bars. They well know that the heart liberated by intoxication opens itself to the effusion of music: music enters the bosoms of men and women, fixes itself there, carries with it the flow of blood, puts dynamism into the whole body, while thought leaps up on the wing of melody. In spite of the implacable color line, through his music the Negro has entered the chapel of hearts and, through his music, the whole fashionable world of balls and drawing rooms—from the working girl to the millionaire's daughter—is delighted.

In our cities we know only the Negro music which has been adapted to the level of our tamed lives. It has to be heard in the midst of the clamor of the skyscrapers and roaring subways.

Let's listen to Louis Armstrong on Broadway, the black Titan of the cry, of the apostrophe, of the burst of laughter, of thunder. He sings, he guffaws, he makes his silver trumpet spurt. He is mathematics, equilibrium on a tightrope. He is Shakespearean! Why not? He only appears at two o'clock, to close the jam session. An assistant has led the orchestra up to now. The orchestra has not been silent for a second. Its precision is staggering. Nothing in our European experience can be compared to it. That implacable exactitude expresses American taste; I see in it an effect of the machine. It is the same thing in university football games; the play is quite different from what it is with us; a stop, a huddle of players, the whistle, then what seems like the explosion of a hand grenade. That lasts a few seconds. The line has or has not been broken through: whistle, stop, and another huddle. Likewise, with Armstrong, the exactitude leads to an unearthly suavity, broken by a blow like a flash of lightning. The men are tireless, like a smoothly running turbine. Sweetness of blue numbers and stridency of hot jazz. When I go to

bed in my hotel room, on the twenty-first floor, I suddenly hear
a police car with its piercing siren, reverberating against the walls
of skyscrapers; kidnapings, the armored cars of banks, gangs with
machine guns and bullet-proof cars, clicking of machines, tough-
ness, speed, cruelty. And the impassive night scarcely disturbed
for an instant: one situation will replace another.

Tap dancers are very popular in the USA—silent Negroes, as
mechanical as a sewing machine, inexhaustible, holding your interest by beating out a rhythmic poem on the stage with the
soles of their shoes. The success of the dance is so precarious that
your breathing is caught up with it. Tap, tap, tap. . . . Imagine a
symphony played by . . . a drum. With the beating of their two
soles they lay a wager. The popularity of tap dancers shows that
the old rhythmic instinct of the virgin African forest has learned
the lesson of the machine and that in America the rigor of exactitude is a pleasure. Idea of a masterpiece: exactitude.

On the stage of Armstrong's night club a series of dances
follow each other, supported by the music and stimulating the
body to frenzied gesticulation. Savagery is constantly present,
particularly in the frightful murder scene which leaves you terri-
fied; these naked Negroes, formidable black athletes, seem as if
they were imported directly from Africa where there are still
tom-toms, massacres, and the complete destruction of villages
or tribes. Is it possible that such memories could survive through
a century of being uprooted? It would seem that only butchery
and agony could call forth such cries, gasps, roars.

An imperial figure, Armstrong makes his entrance. His voice
is as deep as an abyss, it is a black cave. He bursts out laughing,
he roars and puts the trumpet to his mouth. With it he is in
turn demoniac, playful, and massive, from one second to another, in accordance with an astounding fantasy. The man is
extravagantly skillful; he is a king.

Americans, who are not without race prejudice (for deep-
seated reasons), admire their Negroes.

The radio broadcasts the Negro spirit into the home. The

Negroes have virgin ears, a fresh curiosity. The sounds of life echo in them. New sounds, of everything and from everywhere, perhaps ugly or horrible: the grinding of the streetcars, the un-chained madness of the subway, the pounding of machines in factories. From this new uproar around our lives, they make music! Meanwhile, the "conservatories" of Europe teach Gou-nod and Massenet.

Here also new things have sprung up.

In the immense Negro dance hall of Harlem, the Savoy, the ordinary colored people join each other in very nearly savage rites. An ingenious projector throws on the wall behind the orchestra what seem like black strips of broken clouds. In the somber atmosphere, among storm clouds, the music seems to spring from inanimate nature. When I flew over the Atlas Mountains in a plane, I realized that their formation—through erosion, geo-logical dramas, the action of winds—was completely independent of our moral anxieties; man is in a kind of cyclone; he builds solid houses to protect and shelter his heart. Outside, nature is nothing but indifference, even terror. The clouds come from far away, go far away, calm or broken up; sometimes the sky is blue. By itself the grand sport of the sky affects our hearts. Duality appears in the contrast between the unfathomable march of the elements and our precise, careful little calculations, as sublime as they are puerile, established in the heart of the tumult.

In Harlem as on Broadway, the Negro orchestra is impecca-ble, flawless, regular, playing ceaselessly in an ascending rhythm: the trumpet is piercing, strident, screaming over the stamping of feet. It is the equivalent of a beautiful turbine running in the midst of human conversations. Hot jazz.

Jazz, like the skyscrapers, is an *event* and not a deliberately conceived creation. They represent the forces of today. The jazz is more advanced than the architecture. If architecture were at the point reached by jazz, it would be an incredible spectacle. I repeat: Manhattan is hot jazz in stone and steel. The contempo-rary renewal has to attach itself to some point. The Negroes have fixed that point through music. Their simple spirit has caused the reformation to spring up from the depths and has situated it in our own times.

The fundamental revolution in the plastic arts is likewise taking place in music. Through the breach made by cubism, those arts have re-established contact, across time and space, with the high periods. The plastic arts have found again the key to strong expression. There is the same advance in music since mechanical recording makes possible the most fruitful—the most admirable—investigation in every part of the world, everywhere that millenary traditions give us, through folklore, fundamental truths. Today ears and hearts are overwhelmed by these riches. The material gathered together shows high thought in a moving indigence of form—sufficient, popular, human. Records sing in homes. The reformation reaches the very foundation of sensibility. The music of today is failing; the world is being filled with new music: that of machines and that of folklore. The ear receives fresh nourishment. Sensibility is liberated; it is filled up by moving revelations.

They are the foundations of cathedrals of sound which are already rising.

I wish to finish saying what I think about music. The modern world is inundated by it. There is an extravagance of it. Everything takes place to music: dinner, movies, there are radios in homes, cars, at fairs, at automobile, aviation and furniture shows, on steamships at sea, on trains, in bars, and at vacation beach parties; in Sahara camps, in the country of the Foreign Legion, at the poles in the silence of scientific expeditions. The phonograph has brought about this new thing: the record library, the complement of the library of books.

Despairingly professional musicians say: "Music is dying." Likewise, M. Camille Mauclair has written a book with a startling title: *Is Architecture Dying?*

In this matter, as in all the other domains of these stirring times, it should be noted that traditional "music" slips, falls, and is crushed. The Paris Grand Opera, called exactly: National Conservatory of Music, plays *Faust, Samson and Delilah,* to empty red plush seats. With our taxes we pay the heavy expenses of wicker manikins.

Who are those patient, curious, often courageous men who go about the world with mechanical devices in order to record pure music—the music of men—folk music? India, China, Polynesia, Negro and Arabic Africa, Iberian canto jondo, Russian dances, folk songs of the Tyrol, of Bavaria, of the Balkans, of the Carpathians, of Epirus, of Catalonia, of Turkey, Argentinian creole songs, Brazilian songs, rumbas from Martinique. What a harvest! Little by little the museums, the public libraries (slowly), are forming archives. The ear of the world is being filled with great poetry. Musicality is making extraordinary progress. The human spirit is alive.

I return from America; the same evening my wife puts on the record "Fifine," a Parisian *java.* "Listen," she says, "this is something that you will enjoy." Was the absence necessary, the acquisition of new habits, to make clear the architecture of the music of the dance halls of Paris? The exoticism of the "*saetas*" of Seville had had the savor of great discoveries. My ears still full of hot jazz, here I am in the presence of the real originality of the *java;* I find in it mathematical France, precise, exact; I find in it the masses of Paris, a society worthy of interest, so measured, precise, and supple in its thought. A controlled sensuality, a severe ethics.

Throughout the world music escapes the musicians.

Where are the professional musicians? At their concerts, and they are not very gay. So-called "modern" music is nearly always a deliquescence: a kind of contrapuntal noise cleverly combined with the rinsing of bottles and the clatter of glasses. How bored those people are and how they bore us! What is this mandarin's game? They are thoroughly sick inside! The corporation of painters also lives outside the stream of current events.

The schools perpetuate specialists in dead things. Painting and music; architecture also. Music! The modern world vibrates with new sounds. Our ears have become much more sensitive than those of our ancestors. Does the sound of the world have no useful effect on works of art? I shall answer thus: it is a function of our existence; hence it is the very tissue of music. Already Satie and Stravinsky have revealed new harmonies and rhythms. Curious and patient men who record the music of men and who have filled our record albums, there is still a job to do. Record the *sounds of the world*. Engrave mechanically on the record what fashions our ears: the sounds of the street, a symphony. The uproar of crowds at games, at mass meetings, in parades. The companion of so many of us: the cadence, the slight or titanic rhythm of machines at work; on the sea, through the purring of the engines, the sound of the stem cutting into the water, the Aeolian chant of the rigging against the wind, the great voice of the siren. The roar of the airplane, the ticktock of the clocks, the sounding of the hours in silence. The surf of the sea. The Homeric braying of donkeys, the sound of a great speech; the roaring of lions, the song of the nightingale, the rasping of grasshoppers, the chirp of the cricket, the croaking of frogs, the shrill note of tree toads, the barking of dogs at night. What you will. Mechanical devices will isolate for us this immanent music which our thoughtlessness keeps us from hearing. . . .

When the train goes through a tunnel, I am sure that you have been struck by the heroic music that seems to come from inside you; the mechanically precise rhythmic armature formed by the walls of the tunnel is such that you cannot be unaware of the music. As the minutes pass, the cadences vary like the textures of a great symphony. An admirable subject of study for anyone interested in classifying the creative forces which are always available.

I say that Armstrong has recognized these ever-present voices and his genius has put them into music. In an excited Manhattan, the Negroes of the USA have breathed into jazz the song, the rhythm and the sound of machines.

WAX MANIKINS OF FIFTH AVENUE

The wax manikins in the windows of the smart dress shops on Fifth Avenue make women masters, with conquering smiles. Square shoulders, incisive features, sharp coiffure—red hair and green dress, metallic blonde hair and ultramarine blue dress, black hair and red dress.

The Greek coiffure, the Doric and Ionic of Asia Minor, predominates. The face, with its strong features, stands out. The casque is gold, platinum, auburn, sandy, even white.

The manikins in the windows have the heads of Delphic goddesses. Green, lamp-black, red hair. Antique-like heads, here one as if from a tragedy, there one like a Caryatid, Athenas from the Acropolis Museum. Polychromy. When polychromy appears it means that life is breaking out.

Next door I note the funereal entrances of the Empire State Building.

And once again this: that black and those manikins: Aeschylus. Once more this: there are no trees in the city!

One evening, after a dinner with friends, in an active and creative milieu, I thought that I could express my feeling. I astonished my audience. "You have to come a long distance to feel things in that way!"

This magnificent and dominating type of woman does not exist in the USA. It is an ideal. Do the women instinctively feel, through the creative conceptions of dress designers, that they will shine like goddesses? I sense that men, held at a certain distance by the hard labor of their normal life, would thus satisfy the obscure need of their spirits for adoration.

Nevertheless, I have met here two women of this type, one all goodness, the other like Pallas Athena.

Shall I be plunging into the ridiculous if I make the supposition that the people are creating feminine fetishes? For ordinary purposes and for daily use, the little blonds of the movies. To finish off, the vamp—an American invention. Caravaggio and inferiority complexes. Separation, independent lives, lack of contact. All kinds of strange phenomena. Tendency toward pathos. Prose in everyday life, inevitably, except in unusual cases. Consequence: idols on pedestals, fervor—magnificent wax manikins.

In the violent tasks of modern technique, in the superhuman struggle of production, of the Stock Exchange, of business enterprise, Americans are world champions. In the simple, fundamental things of life, *in philosophy*, Americans are only on the way, far from the goal. The contrast is epic. They have a warm aspiration toward wisdom, the result of harmonious cultures; our wisdom, for example. Let's recognize that it is leading us insensibly toward a quiet life of blinders and hearing aids, toward lethargy, and that it has taken away the taste for drama, for strong things, for the great deeds of life . . . unless events born out of life itself break our quietude and launch us, also, away from satisfied egoisms and onto a new and hazardous road.

Is that the only possibility that will enable us to maintain ourselves in the current of life which everywhere blows so impetuously, like a hurricane over the world?

5 NECESSITY OF COMMUNAL PLANS AND ENTERPRISES

THOUGHTS ABOUT FORD

. . . "When the cathedrals were white, collaboration was complete."

I come out of the Ford factories at Detroit. As an architect, I am plunged into a kind of stupor. When I take less than a thousand dollars to a building lot I cannot get even a single room built! Here, for the same money, you can buy a Ford car. The Ford of today combines the most useful automotive developments. All of those mechanical marvels are yours for less than a thousand dollars! On a building lot men work with axes, picks, hammers; they saw, they plane, they work things out well or badly. On one side barbarism, on the other—here at the Ford plant—modern times. I watched the assembly-line production of cars: six thousand cars a day! Unless I am mistaken, a car every forty-five seconds. At the end of the line, a new shift of mechanics comes on. One of them climbs up quickly, sits down, presses the button that starts the line moving. Dejectedly you say to yourself: "It is going to fail! It won't come off!" It never fails. That is the way it is organized. Gleaming, impeccable, without a spot of oil or grease, without even a fingerprint on the shining varnish, the car has slipped by, disappeared. It is born as in a mythological epic, adult at birth! It is launched in life!

That evening, I speak at Cranbrook Academy.

—"This is the dramatic conflict which is strangling architecture, which causes 'building' to remain off the roads of progress. In the Ford factory, everything is collaboration, unity of views, unity of purpose, a perfect convergence of the totality of gestures and ideas. With us, in building, there is nothing but contradictions, hostilities, dispersion, divergence of views, affirmation of opposed purposes, pawing the ground. We pay dearly for it: *building* is a luxury industry and society lives in miserable holes. Or if the general economy bleeds itself white in order to build, a discouraging precariousness nevertheless remains. And the architectural products remain outside the frame of modern times.

"I take a piece of blue chalk and draw the arrow marked (A); I write: *individual liberty*.

"I take a piece of red chalk and draw an arrow marked (B) in the opposite direction; I write: *collective forces*.

"Architecture, upon which these two opposed forces are applied, is immobilized. A paralysis caused by disagreement about purposes. I continue. What is the violet arrow marked (C) which points left? Let's indicate its symbolism by a classical architectural order; I draw a pediment. What is the pediment doing here?

"I have no idea. It is a souvenir of an activity which has been dead for two thousand, a thousand, or five hundred years. But there is the cruel truth that it exists throughout the world—a sign of laziness, of inhibitions, of fears—blocking architecture's way, distorting action, ruining new enterprises. I put in three question marks, since I understand nothing about it, since I have been asking for explanations ever since I opened my eyes on architecture. I have never had an answer.

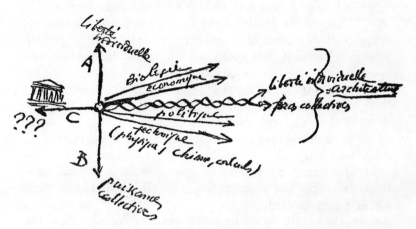

"My three arrows, (A), (B), (C), thus arranged in conflict, not only immobilize architecture, but also make it move backward.

"With the help of Ford, I reason thus:

"Architecture? *The construction of shelters.* For whom? For *men.* That is the program. How express this program in an accessible reality? *By techniques. Make plans.* Plans which are realizable today with existing materials and machines, and which answer the essential needs of man (a psycho-physiological entity). Where are we to bring into concrete reality the potentialities of the plans? In factories. In innumerable workshops under a rigorous industrial control. How are we to breathe spirit into this revolutionary enterprise? By means of architecture, the expression of the spirit of the times. The new times are here.

"Thus a fruitful doctrine is established, on the basis of the living present: (a) program; (b) technique; (c) factories and workshops; (d) architecture and city planning.

"I pick up my colored pieces of chalk again.

"With the blue chalk I draw a twisting arrow which expresses the researches, the gropings, the always anxious advance of discovery—facing the future, turning its back on the past: individual investigation and its most unexpected discoveries.

"With the red chalk I make a similar arrow which is intertwined with the other one: initiatives of small or large groups; mutual helpfulness on a small or large scale; collaboration, co-operation, enthusiasm, the divine madness . . .

"Then, with dark blue, I indicate biology (certitudes).

"With brown, technique (certitudes).

"With green, economics (certitudes).

"With yellow, politics (a precise and rapid instrument of execution).

"This time, architecture is drawn toward a destined synthesis. Necessary and adequate forces of collaboration are in their places, facing forward.

"Let the hitherto contradictory currents line up in a single procession: individual liberty and collective forces in a measured co-operation, the equation of equilibrium.

"Let the ghosts stop blocking the road! Bury them, grave-diggers, bury them please!"

"Ford's experience, repeated in a thousand activities of the modern world, has a lesson for us. Let's accept the lesson. In the name of heaven, let us work usefully for the welfare of men."

THE GREAT WASTE
(From a talk given in Chicago)

. . . "*The measure of our actions is given by the twenty-four-hour solar day.*"

"The fundamental àrgument capable of supporting my proposals for architectural reform and the reorganization of cities, in the eyes of the American public, is the fact that our solar day has been abused. As a result of heedlessness and the insatiable voracity of money, unfortunate initiatives have been followed in urban matters. Work, the immense development of cities—is conducted only for the sake of profit, against the well-being of men. Only the reversal of this false situation can bring *the essential joys*. Equilibrium should reign within the twenty-four-hour solar day, a new equilibrium should be established. Without that, there can be no salvation!

"I express the present solar day, as it exists in the USA and in Europe, by a circle (fig. 1).

"The first eight-hour sector (A) represents sleep. Tomorrow, and each morning, the day will be new and fresh. (B) is an hour and a half lost in transportation—subways, trains, buses, streetcars. (C) represents today the eight hours of work necessary for production. (D) stands for time destroyed in transportation. There is a balance (E) of five leisure hours in the evening: family table, life within the snail shell, the dwelling. What sort of dwelling? Please tell me when, in the ordered day, the day which is the year, the years and all of life, when man, a solid physical animal covered with muscles, animated by the circulation of blood, equipped with a network of nerves, nourished by a respiratory system—when can this living being do for his own subtle and delicate machinery what he is obliged to do for all machines: take care of cleaning, maintenance, repair? Never.

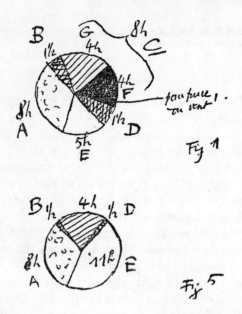

There is no time for that! No provisions are made for that! Tell me, also, when this being who has been organized for millenniums in accordance with the law of the sun, tell me when and where he can expose his pale body to the regenerating rays of the sun? Like a plant in a cave, he lives in darkness. What does he breathe? You know what he breathes! What does he hear? You know the exhausting tumult of contemporary cities. His nerves? Well, they get out of order and are never restored to health.

"I draw (fig. 2) the vague contour which defines the urban region. In the center (M) is the city—business. Industries, workshops, and factories? They are inside the city or around it, in the stupidity of disorder and shortsightedness. The urban region is an immense reservoir; it contains two, three, five, seven, ten million people! It is twelve, eighteen, thirty, sixty miles in diameter. Americans establish new records: the urban regions of New York and Chicago are sixty miles in diameter! What dispersion; why?

What is this frenzy that thrusts millions of beings far away from others? Why? It is because men pursue a chimerical dream; the dream of individual liberty. Because the atrociousness of large cities is such that an instinct of salvation drives everyone to flee, to escape, to pursue the chimera of solitude. The fundamental demand: *liberty*. There are millions who wish once again to walk with their feet in the green grass of nature; who wish to see the sky, clouds against blue; who wish to live with trees, immemorial companions. Millions! They start out, they hurry away, they arrive. Now there are millions grouped together facing a shattered dream! Nature melts away under their feet; it is covered by houses, roads, stations, and grocery stores.

"There are millions of houses. They are garden cities (R), a creation of the late nineteenth century, approved, favored, sanctified by capitalism. Garden cities are the floodgates of the great torrent of accumulated rancors. With this gigantic multitude, with these mountains of claims and demands, they have made dust scattered to the four winds, inert ashes: the dust of men. The egoistic and biased social laws have had their life prolonged as a result.

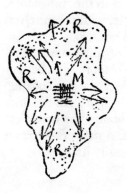

FIG. 2.

FIG. 3.

FIG. 4.

"At the end of the rainbow of disjointed garden cities there is a disappointed dream. When men get home at eight o'clock in the evening their heads and hands are exhausted. They are silent and dead on their feet.

"All collective force has been completely destroyed—the admirable power of action, the lever of enthusiasm, the creator of civic spirit. Society lives in a flat, deadened, flabby way. The sponsors of garden cities and those responsible for the dismembering of cities have loudly proclaimed: "Philanthropy comes first: everyone should have a little garden, a little house of his own, the assurance of freedom." Lies and betrayal of trust! The day has only twenty-four hours. As things are, it is insufficient. It starts over again tomorrow, throughout life. The whole of life has been putrefied by the denaturalization of the city.

"Once again I draw the contour of the urban region (fig. 3). Once again I indicate the city (M). Everything has to be accomplished in twenty-four solar hours: the mad movement of these millions of beings in the circle of their hell. As I have said, transportation systems for the region (P) or the region (X) have been created. First, railroads (S); life in trains: station, coach, station. Then subways (U); then roads (Y)—roads for streetcars, buses, cars, bicycles, and pedestrians. Just think of this: the road passes in front of every one of the houses in the stupendous, fantastic, mad urban region! Please take note, within yourselves, of the incredible network of roads in the urban region.

"Now let's go into one of the houses of this boundless region. With you, in America, there is infinitely more (and better) than with us. There is comfort: electric light, gas for cooking, running water in the sink and bathroom, telephone. All the lines reach out this far. The lines, underground, occupy the boundless region in a network that has to be imagined. A network—over an area sixty miles in diameter—which is immensity itself.

"Fine!

"Who pays for it?

"The question is put squarely. Who pays for it?

"First you reply: 'Work as it is organized in modern times, the very program of our industries and businesses. *Abundance.*'

"Coolly I say: All that goes to *make wind* and nothing more. It brings nothing to anyone, since the passionately sought freedom, the nature you set out to grasp, are only empty air and illusions—a disaster brought about by the unfinished twenty-four-hour day.

"Who pays for it? The State! Where does it get the money? From your pockets. There are crushing taxes, hidden taxes, there are indirect duties on everything that you consume: groceries, shoes, transportation, theater, and motion pictures. . . .

"I understand that the gigantic waste in America and Europe—urban disorganization—constitutes one of the most crushing burdens on modern society. And not the program of its industry and business! A false plan, based on fallacious premises. Freedom? Are you kidding? The slavery of twenty-four voracious hours. That is where you are!

"In conclusion, I take a piece of black chalk and, in the sector of eight hours necessary for production, I cover up one half, half is in black—death. I write: *to make wind.* Trains, Pullmans, subways, cars, roads, and all the service lines, and the administration, and the sales personnel, and the maintenance and repair crews, and the policeman with his stick, all that is the stupid waste of modern times. Every day you, and we, pay for it *with four useless hours of work.*

"No longer is there an aureole around the dollar. No longer are there floods of gold in the USA. After the tragic tomorrows which followed the euphoria stimulated by the last war boom,[1] Americans, feeling their way, tried to become realists; where is the flaw in the system, then, where is the new path? They have become hard as they struggle to save a few pennies from the waste; a few pennies in order to live!

"The production which is useful to society consists of shoes,

1 Written in 1935.

clothes, food and drink, dwellings (shelter in general), books, motion pictures, the theater, works of art. The rest is nothing but wind: a hurricane over the world—*the great waste.*

"The verdict has been spoken. Let's make a constructive proposal, let's establish the program proper to the new times: the reconstruction of urban regions, the vitalization of the country.

"On the same scale, I draw the modern city (fig. 4). There are no suburbs. Modern techniques make it possible to gain in height what is lost in extent. The city is small, compact. The question of transportation resolves itself. People rediscover their feet. With housing units one hundred and sixty-five feet in height, we can accommodate four hundred persons on each one-acre area, *a maximum density.* The units cover only 12 per cent of the ground; the remaining 88 per cent is park; there are fields for sport; *grounds for sport are outside the door.* At the edge, the city rises up vertically beside fields of grain, prairies and orchards. The country is all around; it has entered into the city and made it a "green city" (K). The city is arranged in accordance with its various functions. The country is all around it (L). Cars—the one and a half million cars daily of New York—are an illness, a cancer. Cars will be valuable for week ends or even for daily excursions into the delicate verdure of nature, a few steps away.

"I conclude; I draw a new twenty-four-hour solar circle (fig. 5). Eight hours of sleep (A); a half-hour in transportation (B); four hours of productive work necessary (and sufficient) for production; machines effect their miracle (C); a half-hour in transportation (D). Thus there are eleven hours of leisure every day.

"The *great waste* in America has enabled me to get to the very bottom of the contemporary situation, to see it more clearly than in Europe where there is a similar illness. I see clearly. I understand.

"*These two disks, which represent the solar day, express quite simply the past and the future.*

"I should like to give these eleven hours of leisure another name: *the true working day of machine civilization*. Disinterested work, without regard for profit, the gift of self; care of the body—splendor of the body; solid morality; an ethic. Freely chosen individual occupations. Free participation of individuals in various collective enterprises or games. Society set in movement by all its motors: the individual and the collective in the just and well-proportioned measure which is in the very play of natural forces—the tension between two poles. Mass exists between two poles; one pole, taken by itself, tends toward zero; extremes kill life; life flows in the middle, in the golden mean. Equilibrium is the sign of imperishable movement. Equilibrium is not sleep, ankylosis, lethargy, or death. Equilibrium is the place of union of all forces. Unanimity.

"That is the way the city planner reads the destiny of societies today."

In the USA, on such individual bases, I was able to propose to my listeners the great reform of their cities: the reorganization of the physical machinery of countries, *for the sake of men*. At the same time, it is a program of *great works* and consequently the salvation of industry which must be directed toward fruitful ends.

That is how the adventure shapes up.

The world must be plunged into the adventure!

Plunge people into the adventure! . . . Strong spirits may wish to play the game. But the others? They will shudder in every limb.

Then let the strong spirits invent the catapult designed to plunge everyone into the adventure. Everything will be new. The people in the water! They will have to swim; they will swim; they will have to get out of it and thus reach the new bank.

On the return trip my table companion said to me: "Obviously, if the builders of the cathedrals were to spring up out of the distant past, in modern Paris, they could very well exclaim: 'What, with your various steels—soft, hard, chrome and still others—your artificial Portland cement or electric cement, with your lifting machines, drills, excavators, transporting devices, with your mathematics, your knowledge of physics, chemistry, statics, dynamics, why, good God! you have done nothing worthy and human! You make nothing around you that is luminous! With small stones patiently cut and adjusted to each other without cement, we made cathedrals!' "

THE AUTHORITIES ARE BADLY INFORMED

I had dinner and spent four hours talking to a government official at the home of a mutual friend who is one of the leading architects in America. We had agreed to discuss the problems of contemporary city planning.

I made my own position clear: thus far I have never had anything to do with politics; I am an artisan. I make plans. An inventor's attitude is different from that of a politician. The investigator is absorbed in the search for the reason for things and the search for the relations of men with their milieu. His destiny is to discover, to know and create. To seek and, consequently, to doubt. To make more perfect and, consequently, to change. On his side, the politician keeps himself informed, chooses and executes. He brings different virtues into play. He is part of an equation that is much shorter than that of a discoverer.

I have traveled through most of the world. I have seen the men of the USSR, of Germany, of Italy, of the USA, and of all the other more quiet countries.[1] I realize that the most gigantic enterprise in the world, the USA, has no sound technical plan and no ethical certitude. That verdict came to me through architecture and city planning. It is up to us to study the problem carefully, to arrive at conclusions and, after mature reflection, to suggest *plans* to responsible leaders.

For a long time I have had many opportunities to meet leaders. I am astonished to see—I always judge on the basis of things in my craft—the inconsistency of their information, the uncertainty of their convictions, the tragic deficiency of their decisions. *What is the crucial question for them?* Where is its sounding board? A question is scarcely broached before its various aspects become external facets which are like mirrors of opinion. Decisions are not made on the basis of the objective facts in themselves, in accordance with the line of their movement and development; decisions are made in order "to avoid unfavorable publicity," in order "to square accounts" with X in the opposition group, as a favor to one's relatives or friends. But *appropriate measures?* That is, things hacked out of the reality of the materials and circumstances? They aren't taken! *You would lose your job!* Whether you are a mayor, a Representative, a cabinet officer, or an agent of the people, you are looking for an exit—an honorable one—but not an avenue, an artery to break up, to clear, to put in order—a road leading to the new times. The amount of courage is in proportion to the legitimate necessity of avoiding the loss of the job. The USSR created an admirable phrase: "The main line . . ." "It is in the main line of development. . . ." "It is not in the main line of development. . . ." The men were not up to the ideal; in some cases they fell very low. In architecture and city planning, for instance, they allowed themselves to sink and choke in the most treacherous and execrable quicksands. Disaster, treason, a slap in the face of the sympathetic élite of the world. To console ourselves we

1 Written in 1935.

say: "A slight, youthful fever. It will pass!" Meanwhile, it is a raging fever!

The official eagerly asks me to explain. I talk about my "radiant city" ideas. I make them more graphic and clear with crayons. The basic thesis, studied for years, has a certain purity. My interlocutor is now delighted, now uneasy; he follows the firm line of the reasoning; with me he sees the fans that open out at the crossroads of the idea onto a stream of consequences. He is so sincere, so serious, so full of a sense of responsibility that he reacts in all his being. I am serenely at home in my pure and true system. But his head swarms with orders given, with orders to be issued tomorrow morning, with terrible decisions to be made in a month, in six months; every one of his actions upsets customary procedures, shifts enormous sums of money, enriching some, ruining others. A perilous and inescapable position! I know these leaders! They are all in inextricable positions! He stops me: "Excuse me, but if I did what you suggest, well, to-morrow . . ." etc. . . .

"But, my dear sir, admit that now you are talking politics. Your argument is political. I am talking about the *plan*, the central idea, the trajectory, the direction. You are the artilleryman who fires the gun at the proper moment, but the plan is the objective at which you are shooting. First you have to know what you are shooting at. Then fire."—"True. Our life is confused; we are gasping wildly."—"A page is turning; humanity is abandoning a civilization, is being caught up in machine civilization. It is a revolution and not an evolution; we are moving out immediately and moving in tomorrow. Living from day to day is no longer enough, its incoherence crushes our enterprises. Consider: your American cities are mortally ill. Your social tone is disturbed by the effects of the progressive and finally catastrophic denaturalization of the urban situation. During the euphoria of prosperity (artificial), your industries made all kinds of stupid things. There is a crushing waste in the USA: a mad, sterile tumult. There are tornadoes of dollars, but they no longer go into your pockets—that is, into peoples' stomachs, spirits, or hearts. It was necessary to stop everything, that everything stop! With an admirable energy, the Government is doing everything that it can to drive back the harbingers of death; throughout the country it has initiated vast public works; to overcome the slums, it is having new urban quarters built, with four-story units. The United States needs five million dwelling units. Well, if the cities in the United States carry out their reconstruction on a four-story basis, they will be lost! It is a basic, fundamental error. I tell you that as an architect and city planner. It was recognized that sprawling garden cities were a mistake; it was realized that the skyscrapers of New York and Chicago had killed circulation. It was decided—rather hastily!—that four-story buildings would solve the problem. I say that with four-story constructions cars will not be able to circulate and that the coming leisure of machine civilization will find nothing to work with, neither sites nor buildings. And that building on a four-story scale is discouragingly retrogressive. And that such a dogma, promulgated by important officials, is emphatically a mistake. At the very moment of modern society's great metamorphosis, badly informed authorities make decisions which run counter to the very nature of the circumstances. It is agonizing."

My slight experience with government officials is that they are not well informed. They do not have the time to keep themselves informed and reflect.

If only one of them had an interest in this matter, a genius for it—if he were, so to speak, the Colbert of today—that would be enough. A well-informed man, strong in his convictions, passionate, breaks through obstacles. He would enlighten his colleagues, he would carry them along with him. It is a question of love. That is all there is to it! Loving with all his being a great constructive idea and having freedom of mind and being above easy props, knowing how to create, to look ahead, to build the scaffolding of tomorrow. And may those who look back be turned into statues of salt, as happened once before at Sodom!

Another of our table conversations on board ship: we were completely different beings and thoroughly good friends. A precise and daring surgeon (extraordinarily daring, apparently), imbued with a strong and implacable morality—a Canadian. Then an important industrialist, all of whose reactions reveal that he is a bourgeois, but I notice that he is open to rational and altruistic conceptions. He is French, and a practicing Catholic. Finally, an architect and city planner who is now crushed, now suddenly exalted by being called a poet!

We talk about the USSR. My companions have no leanings toward Soviet experiments. We admit that, everything considered, nothing can be "new," in spite of the dazzling fruits of modern techniques. That there are only ineluctable consequences. But—and this is where our reflection makes sense: the first man is shocked by the USSR, the second is not attracted to it in any way, the third, having been there several times, tells what he experienced. The only useful and true conclusion, which sums up the whole thing, and which developed spontaneously and unanimously is this: *Nothing can be new, except this fact (which is everything): a + sign controls society in the USSR and not a − sign.*

What our societies need, depressed and putrefied as they are by the effect of money, is the + sign inscribed in the bottom of every heart. That is enough, that is everything. It is hope. Hope is enough to make the days radiant. That is the conquest that remains to be made.

Lunch with the assistant police commissioner of New York, at Police Headquarters on Center Street:

"Well, sir, you carry on your shoulders the heaviest load in New York: policing the city, the insoluble problem of circulation, public health."

"The commissioner presides over receptions at City Hall, while in our offices there is an endless procession of messy jobs caused by the problems of the city."

"A million and a half cars every day in a city designed for horse and buggy traffic. Please pass me the menu." On the back I sketch the only possible solution of the modern city's traffic problem:

If we continue to build housing based on a central stairway serving two (or even four) apartments on each floor, the number of persons accommodated *is too small. There are too many house doors*; and since the purpose of a car is *to take you to the door*, the street will be carried along from door to door, *at the foot of the houses*, ad infinitum. The houses will be on a street flanked by two sidewalks. And the fate of the pedestrian will be bound up with that of the motorcar: cars and pedestrians will be in the same bed: *two miles an hour and sixty miles an hour mixed up together, helter-skelter.* The senseless folly of today.

The lot of the pedestrian must be separated from that of the car. That is the problem.

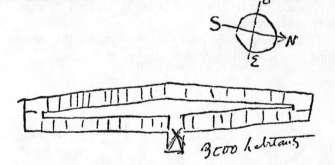

Let's build housing units large enough to accommodate from twenty-five hundred to three thousand people. Elevators and "interior streets." Such a construction represents a "housing unit." There it is possible to organize the "common services," *which are the key of the new domestic economy.*

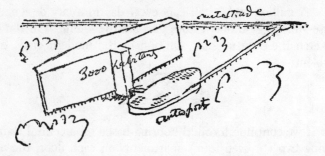

If three thousand persons enter through one door, the next door will be far away. And so on. That is the solution! The autoport, for the arrival, departure, and parking of cars spreads out in front of the door of the housing unit. A branch road connects the autoport with the nearest highway. Autoports and highways are twenty feet above the ground. The housing unit is also twenty feet above the ground, raised up on piles. Nothing encumbers the ground; all of the ground is for pedestrians: 100 per cent of the ground for pedestrians, cars up in the air, separation of pedestrians and cars. The pedestrian, moving two miles an hour, left in peace, cars free to travel at full speed, sixty miles an hour, ninety miles an hour. . . .

One principal remains to be emphasized: the necessity of having a sufficient density in urban agglomerations.

It is our particular folly to meet the problem of concentration which the city—by definition—implies, with village or small town densities: 20, 50 persons per acre. Construction takes up 12 per cent of the ground, 88 per cent is free for parks and

fields for sport, one of the keys to the problem of leisure time
in the future. . . .

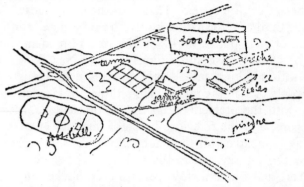

And here is the city reorganized in its normal and harmonious cellular state, *the city in the service of men.* The disappear-
ance of the city of horror . . .

"Then the present cities must be demolished?"

"I'll draw the two transformations which New York has
already accomplished and the third which remains to be accomplished for the salvation of the city."

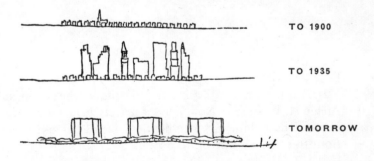

TO 1900

TO 1935

TOMORROW

Up to 1900, the standard city of everywhere and always,
before the development of fast machines. Up to 1935, the spring-
ing up of modern technique: the conquest of height. The sky-

scrapers are too small and the tiny houses remain at the foot of the skyscrapers. A modern metabolic change imposed on a pre-machine age cardiac system. That is the agony of today.

The third transformation involves a wise and well-considered program of great public works, on the scale of modern times.

The amiable assistant commissioner of New York looked at me with admiring and slightly quizzical eyes. He is a frank man; we shook hands cordially. He returned to Headquarters to wrestle with the problems of gangsters, tuberculosis, accidents, traffic jams, and the ferocious horde of financial interests. The next day I embarked for the return trip to Paris, the city roofed over by the gay sky, where the malady is the same as it is in New York and where there is perhaps even blacker uncertainty, since most of our administrators are unaware of Manhattan, the fairy catastrophe which is the laboratory of the new times.

WHAT IS THE AMERICAN PROBLEM?

Dear Mr. Stowell:

Here is the article you asked me to write for the American Architect. Written in New York, it reflects vividly the major impressions and the major certainties which I felt and retain from this first visit in the U.S.A.

I spoke of it on the radio three days after my arrival: From Quarantine, the town appeared to me, in the morning haze, like the promised city—distant, azure and mother-of-pearl, with its spires thrust up toward the sky. This is the Land of the New Times and this is its fantastic and mystic city: the temple of the New World! Then the ship approached Wall Street, it moved past the docks; I exclaimed to myself: "What brutality and what savagery!" But so much explosive force here in the hard geometry of disordered prisms did not displease me. Coming from France at the flat end of 1935, I had confidence.

I saw the skyscrapers, a spectacle which Americans have stopped looking at and to which, after six weeks, I became passively accustomed, like everyone else. A thousand feet of height is an architectural event; in the category of psycho-physiological sensations, it is something important. It takes hold of your throat and viscera. A thing beautiful in itself.

Nevertheless, your mind is disturbed. I said: "The sky-

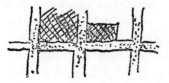

une divagation romantique

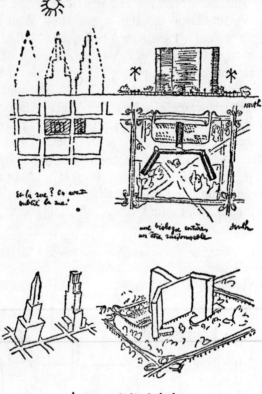

Et la rue? On avait oublié la rue!

une biologie certaine, un être raisonnable

north

south

re-formation cellulaire de la ville

scrapers of New York are too small." And the *New York Herald Tribune* made a headline of it. I explained what I meant. The skyscrapers of New York are romantic: a gesture of pride, and that has importance of course. It is also proof: proof that it is possible to build thousand-foot structures in which the circulation of masses of people from top to bottom is admirably taken care of. But the street has been killed and the city made into a madhouse. They are irrational from top to bottom and the reason for that is a quite absurd zoning regulation. It is disturbing that people in authority should have entertained such ideas and passed ordinances accordingly. Nevertheless, the most recent skyscraper tried to avoid that error and it is a foretaste of the future skyscraper: the rational skyscraper. Then we shall cease to be embarrassed by this new architectural phenomenon, and we shall use it to bring order, rationality, and splendor to New York.

There is violence in the city. But first let's recognize and remember that the principle on which the streets were planned is clear, useful, simple, true, human, and excellent. You are admirably oriented in New York and Manhattan was well designed. In horse and buggy days! The period of the car has come; it is here with its tragic consequences: circulation in New York is hopelessly clogged.

I could never have imagined such a violent, such a decisive, such a simple and also such a diversified arrangement of the

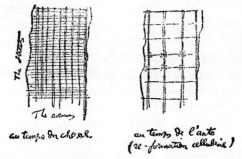

ground of a city. The eight or nine longitudinal avenues mark off the character of areas in a quickly changing gamut which runs from the hideous to the luxurious. Manhattan—a kind of sole stretched out on a rock—has value only along its spinal column; the borders are slums. On foot, you can walk across town in twenty minutes and see that spectacle of contrasts. But what satisfaction can rationality find in it? The borders—the East River and the Hudson—are inaccessible! The sea is inaccessible, invisible. Looking at the plan of New York or an airplane view, you think: "It is certainly the best organized city in the world."

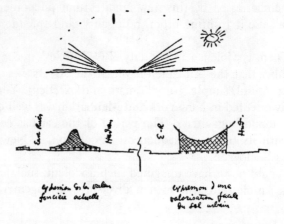

Well, the sea and the vast rivers are invisible and no one gets the benefit of their beauty, their spaciousness, their movement, the splendid play of light on the water! New York, an immense seaport, is as landlocked for its inhabitants as Moscow! And the admirable terrain, seemingly destined to be taken up by immense apartments with windows opening on space, that terrain is desolating: it is filled with slums! A well-managed municipal operation could easily restore the value of those sections and the profit would make it possible to do something about the rest of the city, which is in violent disorder. It astounds a visitor to learn that Manhattan, bristling with skyscrapers, has an average building height of four and one-half stories. Do you realize that: *four and one-half stories?* But it is the imperative and revealing statistical fact which brings hope for the success of a transforming plan capable of establishing order in the city.

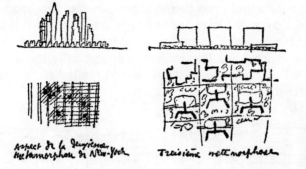

Aspect de la deuxième
métamorphose de New-York

Troisième métamorphose

Here the skyscraper is negative: it kills the street and the city, it has destroyed circulation. More than that, it is a man-eating monster: it sucks the life out of the neighboring areas; it empties them and ruins them. Once again, saving solutions of the urban problem come to mind. The skyscraper is too small and it destroys everything. Make it larger, true and useful: it will restore an immense area of ground, it will pay for the ruined properties, it will give the city verdure and excellent circulation: all the ground in parks for pedestrians and cars up in the air, on elevated roads, a few roads (one-way), permitting a speed of ninety miles an hour and going . . . simply from one skyscraper to another. Collaborative measures are needed to achieve that goal; without them, no salvation is possible! We shall have to think about that someday, through the organization of co-operatives or real-estate syndicates, or through strong and paternal governmental measures (with all the energy of the father who knows what the children should do).

Between the present skyscrapers there are masses of large and small buildings. Most of them small. What are these small houses doing in dramatic Manhattan? I haven't the slightest idea. It is incomprehensible. It is a fact, nothing more, as the debris after an earthquake or bombardment is a fact.

Central Park has a different lesson. Notice how normal and spontaneous it is for the great hotels and large apartment houses

to come there and open their windows on the clear space. But
Central Park is too large and it is a hole in the midst of build-
ings. It is a lesson. You go through Central Park as if you were
in a no man's land. The verdure, and especially the space, of
Central Park should be distributed and multiplied throughout
Manhattan.

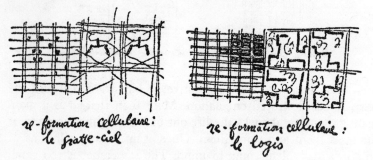

re-formation cellulaire:
le gratte-ciel

re-formation cellulaire:
le logis

The average building height in New York is four and one-
half stories. With only sixteen stories, it could regain three-
fourths of its ground: Central Park for everyone, parks at the
foot of the buildings, sport at the foot of the buildings. And
the buildings in the city and not in Connecticut! But that is
another story.

It is the story of the New Yorker in his mad pursuit of
imaginary paradises.

It is the main story of the USA and it is worth stopping
to consider. Thus you go on to speak about New York and Chicago and all the large and small cities which spring up everywhere in the country on the same pattern and in the same disorder and which, someday—who knows?—will be other New
Yorks and other Chicagos.

To speak fairly, let's first recognize that Chicago has dazzling
drives along the shore with splendid apartment houses facing
the lake and parks; that New York has fine apartment buildings
here and there, and delightful villas in distant and not very
accessible suburbs.

Also, that those who live in these apartments and villas are "important people" and that—in general—having kept their fortune (the family fortune) they think that things are all right as they are. On my side, I think a good deal about the crowds in the subways who return in the evening to lodgings that are not like paradise. Millions of beings whose lives are without hope, without means of repose—without sky, without sun, without verdure.

In the name of those crowds, I can say that things are not all right! But, for the moment, those crowds have nothing to say. How long will that last?

Behind the drives of Chicago there are slums, immediately behind them, a few feet away. And what slums! An immense area, a world of slums!

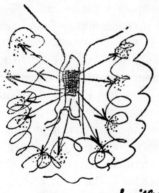

la Dislocation de la ville;
maïnance du cancer

Let's try to see through the suburban illusions of American cities.

Manhattan is a city so hostile to the most fundamental needs of the human spirit that the dream of escape fixes itself in every heart. Get away! Avoid dissipating your life, the life of your family, in the midst of this implacable hardness. To be able to open your eyes on a patch of sky, to live near a tree, beside a lawn. And to flee forever from the noise, the confusion of the city.

This measureless dream has materialized. Millions of city people have set out in search of an illusory country. Reaching it, living in it, they have killed the country. This enormous region, spread out so far around the city, is now suburban. Nothing remains except the dream, the desperate dream of being free, at least master of one's destiny.

Every day it means hours in the subway, on the bus, or in the train. And the loss of all collective life—the sap of a nation. And life has only a very limited liberty, with door beside door, window against window, the road in front of the door, the sky cut off by surrounding roofs, the few trees left after all that. (I am still speaking of those who are not well to do, the masses of people who make up enormous agglomerations like New York and Chicago.)

In my lectures in the USA, I tried to make it clear that that was the fatal American waste, paid for by a new and unconscious slavery. The hours lost in getting to innumerable suburban communities *are nothing by comparison with the daily hours lost by everyone, over and above truly productive work, in order to pay for that mistake!* For the gigantic suburbs, house after house, swallow up an incredibly tangled network of railroads, highways, service lines for water, gas, electricity, telephone. I ask you: who pays for that? We do, you do, everyone does every day, through the tribute of three or four hours of sterile work given in order to pay for those futilities, given by every one of you in order to make wind, in order to find an occasional tree, a little patch of sky, along roads made dangerous by cars. When you can have many trees, a great deal of sky, a vast amount of space and no cars to contend with, if you agree to return to the city, to Manhattan, on condition that you make Manhattan—a vast and quite sufficient area—a "radiant city," that is, a city dedicated to the necessary and satisfying human joys.

um petit aspect de deux millions de rêves:
ceci est capital! la liberté individuelle.

For Manhattan is large enough to accommodate millions of residents and businessmen and workers in delightful conditions, if it is organized in an orderly way.

Manhattan can be put in order by a general rehabilitation of its land, that is, New York can be made the most harmonious city in the world and at the same time yield a profit to those who share in that wise operation. It can give joy to those who, in hours of sterile slavery, pursue the fatal illusion of garden cities.

Americans have proved by significant works that they are capable of undertaking anything when the technical and financial machinery is set in motion. I ask that they set the thinking machine in motion, that is, that they reflect about the acute and fatal illness of New York and Chicago (and other cities) in order to recognize the true evil and in order to find the true remedy. Americans made the Holland Tunnel and the Pulaski Skyway which passes over a complex industrial area—factories, railroads, bodies of water, roads, etc. . . . They made that thing of serene and harmonious splendor which is the George Washington Bridge over the Hudson. They have made parkways (premises of the future city); they were persuaded to build the elevated superhighway beside the Hudson River docks.

In addition, they have made elevators work, something which we have not accomplished in Europe. They have constructed huge blocks of apartment houses which are so well organized and located that they make ideal quarters for the well to do.

Well then:

What is Manhattan? An island bordered by water and space, with an invigorating and healthy climate, an area approximately twelve miles long and two miles wide. Surface area about sixteen thousand acres.

From minute, varied, multiple, and precise studies, I know that it is possible to house 400 persons per acre in excellent living conditions (the conditions of "radiant city": 12 per cent of the ground for buildings, 88 per cent for parks, promenades and sport, separation of pedestrians and cars, 100 per cent of the ground free for pedestrians, sport just outside the door (sport for everyone, every day), great spaces outside each window (600, 1,200 feet) and windows that all get the sun, etc. . . .). I know that Manhattan can house six million persons! . . . That is a certainty.

When there are six million people living in Manhattan, you will be able to get away from dependence on cars and bankrupt railroads and you will work three or four hours less every day because you will no longer have to pay for the waste of garden cities in Connecticut and New Jersey.

Your cars will move through the organized city at sixty or

ninety miles an hour and, in a few minutes, you will be able to
enjoy real country, the spectacle of trees and fields and sky spread
out all around you. And the roads will be rid of those obsessing
green and red lights which today destroy the very principle of
a car, which is to go fast; the road will be free!

To reconstruct American cities and especially Manhattan,
it is first necessary to know that there is a place where the reconstruction can take place. *It is Manhattan, which is large enough
to hold six million persons.*

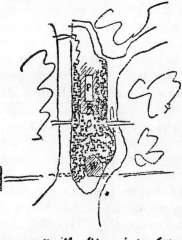

*une nouvelle ville efficace in manhattan:
six million d' habitants*

It is necessary to know whether the existing conditions are
favorable to the realization of the dream of individual liberty
and the natural satisfactions human hearts need: sky, sun, space,
trees. Manhattan is marvelously designed for the materialization
of such dreams . . . immense and empty river banks (yes, empty,
or nearly so). An immense center which is empty or sterile, thus
available, thus an opportunity for investment, between the skyscrapers of Wall Street and 34th Street: a tremendous space in

the heart of the city, a space genuinely suitable for the residential section; residence should be in the center of the city. The bridges are there, the subways are there.

The present streets must be regrouped in larger units. The present street system is too dense. *The street system makes impossible*—I repeat: makes impossible—*any solution of the traffic problem*. It is easy to do, if you know *that it has to be done*.

The means to do it? They are in the city itself, they are the very life of the city. Manhattan is covered with buildings *whose average height is four and one-half stories*. You can see very easily that that is the key to the solution. If you put four hundred persons per acre into Manhattan, you increase the value of land in Manhattan two, three, or four times. With that profit, you will be able to pay the expense of making it work: setting up footpaths for pedestrians and elevated highways. The means are in the very life of the city: the Empire State Building has drained the sap out of the surrounding neighborhood; it has ruined a great many people. Rockefeller Center has done the same and, in turn, has ruined the Empire State Building. The money that you talk about, that you seek, is in the mobile forces of the city, in the city's need to go on living and on better terms. If disorder presides over the operation required to save the New York region, many will be ruined and few will profit. If the necessary measures are recognized as being in the public interest— more than that: in the interest of *public salvation*—the authorities can carry through the transformation and establish, on the basis of a good plan, the wealth and well-being of everyone. But *a good plan* is necessary, a complete, symphonic plan; one that satisfies collective needs and assures individual happiness. *The cellular reformation of American cities is required*. That is the function of powerful and beneficent public authorities: authorities acting as the head of the family.

One thing remains to be emphasized: housing is an essential, urgent, almost unlimited need, in the USA and throughout the world.

A considerable part of New York is nothing more than a provisional city. A city which will be replaced by another city. But everything must be carried out in accordance with the laws and measures of a metamorphosis in keeping with the needs of the times. *Metamorphosis.* That is the word which fixed itself in my mind while I was in the United States. Growth has been relatively regular, though very much accelerated, even precipitous. They were satisfied with city blocks of the type used in horse and buggy colonial days when communities were small. The present dimensions of New York and Chicago are excessive, disproportionate, outside the daily realities imposed on us by the cosmic law of the sun: the twenty-four-hour day. American cities (and Paris and London, and Berlin and Moscow) must be brought back to a form of organization which takes into account the time factor involved in all of our undertakings, all of our constructions, all of our labors: the time between sunrise and sunset (if you prefer: between periods of sleep).

But if housing is a fundamental need in the USA, consideration should be given to the realities and possibilities of machine production. In the USA the coefficient of cost of automobiles as compared with the period before 1914 is —50. That is because production was organized in such a way as to exploit the miracle of machines. The coefficient of cost of buildings as compared with the prewar period is + 210. That is because no advantage was taken of the methods that might have overcome heavy labor costs in the building trades which are essential to the country.

I say that modern techniques prove that *heavy industry can operate in the field of building.* That housing can be and should be made in factories—in plants which are intended only to make sterile consumption goods—superfluous products.

Housing is indispensable for everyone.

Let it be made in factories.

Let's change the cellular arrangement of cities so as to give the new projects the scale and standardization necessary in machine production.

Let industry discover that its real market is in housing.

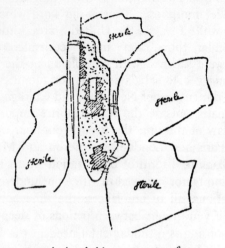

ici un terrain libre ... dans Manhattan

Let's stop the frightful waste of disastrously overextended agglomerations.

Let the public authorities realize that their great task is in *city planning legislation for the United States, productive of a market for industry and of the essential joys of the human heart and body.*

And let's realize the consequences: three or four hours less work every day for everyone. Unemployment? Not at all! Liberation from a completely sterile contribution toward the upkeep of waste—of the tremendous waste of American cities. *Those three or four hours brought nothing to anyone, they paid for nothing but foolishness—air.*

More leisure time then. With the help of machines, four

hours of productive work are sufficient. Places are needed—
buildings and grounds—to make use of the new leisure, so that
it may not result in a new convulsion of contemporary society.
Cities must be designed accordingly, and educational preparation
made for the useful employment of the new hours of freedom
in the development of body and spirit.

I see the machines of the United States and the prodigious
industrial organization of America. I see the well-considered plan
which fixes the program of essential production. I see the end
of the slavery in the USA—in subways, buses, trains, and on roads
—the daily hours lost in *doing nothing*. I see those daily hours
demanded in payment for unnecessary things, over and above
legitimate consumption: shoes, clothes, food, games, and diversions—the senseless expenditures of endlessly expanded cities,
I see those hours canceled out. I see education taking hold of the
spirit, forming opinion, arousing desires, creating a will. And I
see the public authorities properly, radically, profoundly, and
exactly informed about the possibilities of today (its techniques
and needs), finally considering the necessity of undertaking the
great work of reconstructing the cities. Devising the proper legislation, subjugating overdeveloped egoisms to the urgent necessities of public welfare, co-ordinating the powers of life, extracting
useful forces from the vitality of cities and guiding them to where
they should be and where they should act in the service of men.

The man of the machine age standing up over his machines,
using them, making them produce and bringing to realization
the imperative necessity of the new era: the human dwelling,
the radiant dwelling, combining all the benefits of progress, of
organization and of a plan designed in terms of the most profound needs of human nature, sun, sky, space, and trees—essential joys.

REPLY TO A QUESTIONNAIRE

My dear Mr. Percival Goodman:
Your questionnaire rests on the most solid kind of base and one that takes into full account the great and imminent transformation of architecture and city planning.
I am very glad to reply.

QUESTION 1

Do you believe that the future of architecture is in standardization of design and production?
The terminology employed today is no longer exact. The word "architecture" is today more understandable as an idea than as a material fact; "architecture": *to order, to put in order. . . . in a superior way—materially and spiritually, and so on. . . .* This idea touches a great number of activities and concerns many kinds of production: the hull of a ship, a plane, a car, a radio, the group of machines in a power plant . . . do they lack architectural character or are they sustained by architecture? I shall not reply here. But I should like to suggest other terms for the question: (a) *Do you believe that the future of housing and cities is in the standardization of design and production?* And I add this: (b) *Can architecture, understood as superior spiritual intervention, take over the task of establishing standardized designs?*

(a) *Do you believe that the future of housing and cities is in standardization of design and production?*
I am profoundly convinced that it is. That is the cause and result of all my researches in architecture and city planning since 1922 (*A Contemporary City for Three Million People*, Autumn Salon, Paris).

As a foundation for the demonstration a fundamental preliminary postulate must be accepted: *Machine civilization was born over a hundred years ago. During the first period (1830-1930), the machine turned society upside down.* Little by little, it destroyed craft traditions; it stimulated new groups: engineers, chemists, research physicists with practical aims, great numbers of mechanics who constitute a technical élite previously unknown. It created new production programs: machines making machines. The new machines produce rapidly consumption goods of excellent quality, from food to clothing and diversion; another group of machines serves to produce speed; a third produces energy to replace the labor of arms and bodies.

New products, foods, clothes, and pleasures have upset millenary habits of economy, frugality, have aroused new desires, have created henceforth imperative needs.

Speed has made possible the transport of products and persons. Millenary ideas of time and duration have been obliterated and replaced by an entirely new use of the solar day, an unexpected division of labor. The family has been torn apart; society has undergone a violent and relentless bruising; concentrations of productive power have brought about previously unknown concentrations of workers.

Energy (in the form of steam or electricity) has made gigantic enterprises possible in an apparently democratic system, initiatives which were formerly possible only through slavery.

In forty years, through the coming of electricity, the eternal solar rhythm has been disturbed and modified: night is no longer the signal for rest. Far from it. Innumerable activities have sprung up in the conquered night.

Etc. . . .

This tremendous first century of machine civilization has forged the extraordinary body of machinery, unknown before, of a society whose dreams seem always to be realized. The machinery has been created. The necessary forces and powers are here. . . .

But during this period, in the course of this stubborn and

perhaps sublime race (the nineteenth century), everything that constitutes the very fabric of societies was broken and torn apart. Man was disturbed. More than that, he was no longer considered anything but a pair of arms, a unit in the production system. Human equilibrium foundered. A page of human history had been turned. We were projected into a different adventure, a new adventure.

Equilibrium is gone. Everything is collapsing. It is necessary, then, to readjust everything, it is necessary to re-establish a harmony, the harmony. That can be done only on the basis of a fundamental factor—the only factor which can be taken into consideration: respect for men, the happiness of men.

Man dominating machines, commanding machines, demanding of them a lightening of his task, man asking benefits, happiness, harmony, from the gigantic effort which has just been made.

To the fundamental postulate which is to outline our route, I add the conclusion: *the second period of machine civilization has begun, the period of harmony, machines in the service of men.*

That means undertaking the great work of equipping modern society, cities, housing, means of transportation, the disposition of the countryside.

This is my answer to question (a):

THE TASK BEFORE THE SECOND PERIOD OF MACHINE CIVILIZA-
TION—cities and housing—IS SO IMMENSE THAT, QUITE PURELY
AND SIMPLY, IT CONSTITUTES THE NEW AND GIGANTIC PROGRAM
OF INDUSTRIAL PRODUCTION. ITS MARKET IS IN CITIES, HOUSES,
FARMS, AND AGRICULTURAL VILLAGES.

The old methods of building (wood, brick, or stone) involve unsatisfactory procedures and results. Neither machines nor modern methods of organizing work can be used. The advantages of nineteenth- and twentieth-century instruments cannot be exploited. Today, the problem of cities and housing cannot be soundly considered except in terms of the complete participation of large-scale industry. Houses should no longer be built on the lot itself by uncontrolled hand labor under the unfavorable conditions of seasonal inclemencies. I have said that the house, in all its elements from the ground level, should be made in steel workshops, in factories, using metal, wood, or synthetic materials, *as cars are made in series at the factory.*

But what kind of houses and what kind of cities? That is the question.

At present, the experts about cities and houses—the architects—are absorbed in contradictory debates, often academic or sophistical—when time is pressing and when industry, standing by, is waiting for a market.

The debates lead nowhere. Styles, past or modern. That is not the question. The question is this: modern cities in which a man may live serenely, joyously, bring up his family, take care of and train his body, take care of and train his mind, freely enjoy the greatest individual liberty, freely benefit from collective forces. The cosmic twenty-four-hour solar day, in its infallible alternation of night and day, gives all our undertakings the measure of time and, consequently, the measure of distance.

Further, through simple necessity, the automobile should find its proper role; introduced into the city, it has brought utter confusion. Its function should be determined. One goal, among others, is the separation of automobiles and pedestrians. It may be added that the ground should belong to pedestrians, *unencumbered ground.*

Thus, the problem of housing involves that of the city. Architecture and city planning are now one and the same thing. Let's answer question (a) by saying this: Only through the search for useful, efficient, true, and human standards (on the human scale of heart and body—biology and psychology) will industry be able to take hold in the field of building which up to now has remained bound to ruinous methods which reject the gains of technical progress.

And I immediately answer question (b): *Can architecture,*

understood as superior spiritual intervention, play a part in the establishment of standardized designs? with a decisive yes. Dwellings and cities, microcosm and macrocosm, shelters for individual, family, and collective life, the very emanation of the life of a society, of a civilization, require a superior ordering, for the sake of man (biology and psychology) and consequently call upon the architect. But, in this matter, where is the architect and who is he? Once again, that is the question!

I am convinced that it is a question of a new spirit in architecture, of new men or men who have the flexibility, the courage, and the desire to adapt themselves to very new conditions. Those conditions are of two kinds: First, the appropriate response to all truly human needs, needs on every social level; and that involves a basic recasting of dimensions, of plan elements, an extensive knowledge of technical progress, etc. . . ; and here the architect concerned with housing is like a naturalist—he becomes a kind of savant who studies "the animal called man" (physiology and psychology); second, a proper understanding of all the imperative though infinitely supple demands of industrial production; and that means attentive contact with the world of industry, labor, materials, and organization, etc. . . . ; and here the architect is like the engineer; a severe form of thinking is demanded of him.

Finally, he is more than ever an "architect." He is an architect like those who built the "houses" of earlier days in which everything was present: the best techniques, the most efficient, desirable, fruitful, and economical dimensions and plans, in which wisdom was in control and expressed itself through poetry. In those periods, the word "architect" was not used. The house was a product of collective efforts, the house was folklore (the houses of all countries and civilizations, until the Schools developed and, with them, academism).

QUESTION 2

If your answer is in the affirmative, does that mean techno-

logical unemployment for architects or will the immense field opened up by the "science of shelter" provide work for everyone?

The answer depends simply on the quality of the professional men concerned, the architects themselves. There are some of them for whom "it is too late," but they will console themselves by doing a considerable number of traditional works in the period of evolution of the new cities and housing.

From personal experience, I believe that the new tasks demand of us a limitless vigilance, devotion, curiosity, constancy, and imagination.

Nothing is easier than hitting on an accidentally effective style. When you are confronted with the question of a standard, you find pitfalls and obstacles at every step: the difficulty is immense and almost beyond the powers of a single man. The problem is to see what standard is in question and what may properly be standardized. That is research whose conclusions can lead housing and cities to their ruin through inhumanity and oppressive boredom, or can, on the contrary, bring grace, variety, suppleness, and the infinite manifestations of personality (though that is bounded by limits "naturally" much more restricted than is imagined by those who have an unfortunate tendency to talk without having reflected about the question or without having observed, in time and space, the magnificent and humanly determined standards left as witnesses of human dignity and propriety: those standards, from folklore, are the basic expression of what is necessary and sufficient).

I think, then, that the "science of shelter," as you call it, demands a new spirit and consequently those who are animated by it. And not only the young can be animated by it.

QUESTION 3

If there should be a "science of shelter," how will the architect be able to prepare himself in that science, for the sake of his work? Do you believe that the present system of architectural education is in any way suitable to these new problems? Will

*there be a more intimate collaboration between the architect
and other technicians than there has been up to now?*

That is a question that is a question! It is the crucial problem of architectural education. I feel that I am in a particularly
hazardous and special situation which makes it difficult for me
to answer. I have never been able to accept the instruction of the
schools for the simple reason that I have a bad character, but
more especially because I built my first house, from "a" to "z"
(very finished and complicated), at the age of eighteen. From
my youth I have had the weight of stone and brick in my arms,
the astonishing resistance of wood in my eyes, the miraculous
qualities of metal in my mind, etc. . . . And I have long felt that,
on the design sheet, there are designs and designs! That is, that
the same spaces and the same thicknesses, according as they are to
be worked out in stone, brick, wood, or iron, have different potentialities, powers that touch feeling as strongly marked as their
physical powers, in a word, that in the matter of architecture, permanent contact with matter (with the materials) is a fundamental necessity. Today, as always, I continue to marvel at the
unexpected resources of matter. I even feel that the new phenomena of construction are going to be found in those resources
which we know only in part, in a rough way. Here, then, when
we are in daily contact with industry (workshop and engineers),
we shall acquire wings and we shall discover in these phenomena
of construction, architecture, that is, the harmonious and proportioned disposition of materials used for the sake of creating
living works.

Harmonious and proportioned: that raises the level of discussion, places it on another plane. We must cultivate in ourselves all the capacities, all the natural gifts that we may have in
that subjective domain which leads to the miracle of beauty.
Beauty, the mathematical locus of harmony. Proportion? What
is it? The *nothing* which is *everything* and which makes things
smile.

How useful it is to enlighten professional architects about

that eminent attribute of architecture. To enlighten minds about the radiant powers of divine proportion. In the precise discussion stimulated by your questionnaire, allow me to open the window on the unlimited horizons of art. Art, that is, *the way of doing things*. It is here that individual responsibility enters in and that is what we have to talk about in connection with the prospective development of a standard: no standard is acceptable unless it is the expression of grace. In the religious sense, grace means everything. *I consider that he who is not conscious of grace does not have the right to become an architect.* And consequently, I should begin the preparatory researches for this vocation *on the ground of proportion*, something for which one has or has not a gift. It is enough to recognize it at the start; systematic methods can lead to a verdict and make it possible to turn aside from the vocation those who do not have the fundamental qualifications: imagination, poetry, and plastic intelligence.

QUESTION 4

If your answer is in the negative, what do you think the future of architects and architecture will be?

The third question seems to me a good question, but the fourth one strikes me as superfluous. The future of architecture is not in doubt: all the countries in the world have to fit themselves out completely and with an infinitely more voluminous mass of things than ever before. In passing, let's once more salute the foolish book by M. Camille Mauclair: *Is Architecture Dying?*

That clarifies the debate. What is this prophet of disaster talking about? About "architecture" considered as an activity which today is in decline. Not as the noble and necessary duty of constructing the new times whose realization can bring "the essential joys" to men through the organization of cities and fields. This dying "architecture" was only one of the forms of the twilight which is falling on the end of a civilization. In this "architecture" there were good intentions, but also all the malignant forms in which vanity, stupidity, waste, laziness, and money are enthroned. Yes, that "architecture" is dead. Decked out with striped plumes, embroidery, and decorations, made up entirely of pretenses, it triumphed in the nineteenth and twentieth centuries and killed the *sense of architecture*. It was nothing but a circus parade. Here and now I should like to set up the true image of architecture, *of the idea of a materially and spiritually superior putting-in-order*.

For that purpose it is enough to designate the domains which such a superior ordering is able to master. Housing, the "science of shelter" as you call it, can be completely dominated by that lofty point of view. And from the beginning, at the very birth of the city, that is, in city planning, at the precise moment when plans conceived by a *feeling heart* on the basis of austere economic, technical, and sociological data, determine forever the nobility and joy which flow from them. And, among these plans which, alas, can be miserable as well as magnificent, among these plans which are the ordering of the city, its composition, the immediate and future grace of its development, proportions which are hideous or delightful, other urban elements will enter in whose significance is different from that of housing or the "science of shelter." They will be, like the themes of a fugue in a cantata by Bach, the important monuments of the city: the civic center, the business center. Here will stand buildings different from the housing units, having a different biology: civic buildings, city halls, theaters, numerous places for diversion or study. With such a varied biology, architectural form also will be varied. But the spirit which will animate the whole complex arrangement, should it be, could it be, other than the spirit which has given order to the city itself and to life itself, in the residential sections, in a materially and spiritually *superior* way? There can be nothing in it which is not part of a *unity*. Here, by their very nature, the works will call less upon organized groups of the new technicians of the "science of shelter"; they will call for more strongly endowed individuals, working in a more isolated way, creating a harmonious body of work under the direction and guidance of one or of several authoritative and concordant individuals.

Thus there will be brilliant accents in the city, places marked by strong intelligence, even genius. There are exceptional places and roles which are difficult for architecture and architects. This needed to be said in order to make it clear that, though housing is going to bring together large teams of specialists concerned with "habitation," the field of architecture remains larger than ever. And without taking the time here to explain in detail, I may add that there are other tasks whose harmonious realization can be magnificently *architectural*: highways, viaducts, autoports, airports, stations, and vehicles.

QUESTION 5

Do you think that, in any consideration of the future of architecture, the fundamental question to be asked is: What will the prevailing economic system be? And if so, under what economic system will architecture prosper most?

This question touches upon ideas which my constant study of architecture and city planning has led me to answer by a very clear principle and attitude in the face of today's confusion and chaos:

The plan is dictator! Let each specialist establish the plans which are in conformity with the new times, let him get at the problem in that way, let him go to the heart of the question, let him find out what it is materially and spiritually possible to do now. This magnificent and fertile work of preparation, these *plans* are the ones which will answer all questions, they will indicate the measures to be taken, the laws to be made, the men to be placed in useful posts. Today, in all countries, the same sterile complaint is the answer to accumulated evils: "We don't have the necessary laws . . . the regulations don't allow it . . . , property interests are antagonistic . . . , it is useless to think of anything new, strong, true . . . , circumstances are unfavorable."

The circumstances must be attacked, then, but attacked in a specific way. And for that purpose, one must be capable of the optimism which consists in drawing up on paper the precise and *technically* feasible plans which are to transform the present misery into tomorrow's happiness.

Once these plans are made, discussion is closed, doubt swept away, certainty assured: *here is what can be done immediately.* Here are New York and Chicago, and Paris and Moscow as they should be. There is no imaginable régime which can ignore *plans.* What exists and crushes us today? Only various kinds of régimes: USA, England, France, Italy, Germany, USSR, and others, yet, in spite of diversity and opposed doctrines, everywhere there is confusion and error because of a lack of plans (for which we hear comically acrobatic excuses and pretexts). The technicians have not done their duty. The various régimes (whatever they may be) *are not well informed, they do not know where they are going* (in the domain which concerns us). Seen from the planet Mars, they would appear to be idly turning machines, without raw materials: *plans for the equipping of machine civilization have not been worked out.*

I intend to stand on the terrain of *plan;* feet solidly on the ground, I am able to affirm serenely that certain reforms are necessary, that certain steps should be taken. The plans demonstrate that to assure the benefits of individual liberty, to nourish collective powers, to bring to an end the frenzied waste of contemporary urban agglomerations, it is necessary to prepare for the execution of communal enterprises. Has it ever been otherwise in the great periods? The difference today is that millions of beings injured by negligence and egoism must be rescued from misfortune. Build housing, reform the cellular system of cities, equip the countries of the world, that is our task. That is the program for society in the new era of machine civilization. That is bread on the table, work for everyone, the program of general activities for all countries.

IN THE CALENDAR OF THE WORLD

Money is "fast," the Americans are slow. The country is daring, the Americans are timid. The enterprises are bold, the Americans are afraid. The skyscrapers are greater than the architects. The events are stronger than the men. The USA is immense, the program is insatiable. Those who venture to think subtly (with finesse) and to feel subtly, do not yet find an echo: they are pushed aside. Those who enjoy art are outside the general circuit. The great ladies attack, but are forced to retreat. Women are Amazons. Cocktail parties are a safety-valve: crowds of people standing up. They are full of life, they are afraid of life. The radio, the Sunday *New York Times*, Pullman cars, fill up the voids and empty spaces. And yet, no philosophy of life appears—of life, of enjoyment, of the joining together of the idea and its resolution in an accomplished act. America is young. They do not taste, they do not savor—they drink. Not a great deal has been accomplished, but everything is possible, everything is hope, expectation, approaching certainty. What power! Let's make a judgment: Young people are anxious, melancholy, sad, and turbulent. Old people, sometimes, are the ones who become young, know, are aware, act, believe, and are gay. And get things done.

When I am in the Place de l'Opéra in Paris, am I in the navel of the world? No, it's finished; I feel myself far away, elsewhere, and the world has also abandoned this center which is no longer anything but the ghost of a spent civilization.

I left for New York without having the slightest idea of what I would find there. I saw a mass striving for distinction and intermittently experiencing defeats and victories; money projects them in an inhuman jazz which would be sterile if it did not determine, by the scope of its tasks, the dimensions of modern times.

I returned to Paris and found mediocre bistros, but also the sky everywhere over the city and the grace of proportion and the care given to every detail for the sake of true pleasure. In the springtime, the sap of the country flowed more spontaneously and fully than I had imagined it would. Curtains torn away, masquerades put aside—the profound reason for life's undertakings was rediscovered: the dignity of man, man made manifest by the masses, profound and full of ancestral culture; the masses that enter into the spirit of things like a flood.

In all the stubborn attempts to which I have dedicated myself—the equipping of machine civilization—I have been told, in spite of emphatic and well justified protests: "We are too old!" You are not old because you have lived for two thousand years! You have simply reached your majority. Mature things can be done. It is time for them.

The USA is young, very young, at the age of Olympic champion: with a handsome shock of hair on an athletic body, with a youthful heart, at once strong and weak. But keep it clearly in mind that this is the country which raised up Manhattan into the sky. And if you dislike it, you are wrong. You should recognize what it has done and go to see it.

A page of human history is turning and the world is upside down. The last orgies of Moloch—of filthy money—soil everything that is pure and creative. It is a universal event; it carries with it all the inhabited parts of the earth. Speculative, elevated, disinterested, sublime ideas are smoldering in the East—India, China —and have given the Russians the power of sacrificial resistance. But the whole world opens itself to renewal. There are mistakes, extravagances, diverse points of departure. Everywhere there is an immense hope. And at the same time, all the doors seem to be closing everywhere: defenses are thrown up because an attack is being made. Everywhere all the doors are opening. In an effort to see clearly, a general classification is taking place. When you

attempt a classification, you are often relegated to some confining and out of the way spot, but you will get away and recapture
your destiny, which is to be this or that among the various possibilities and to act in this way or that way, in accordance with
your destiny.

In the calendar of the world, the USA and the USSR are
the two great systems which are truly new and whose products
are revolutionary. Each country offers an admirable—and disconcerting—spectacle. There you realize the fated length of successive
days: everything cannot be done at once and, to go forward
effectively, it is sometimes necessary to fall back. In the sure
advance before our eyes, there are withdrawals—perhaps momen-
tary—which seem to us as high as the Himalayas and which, consequently, discourage us. Time will take care of that. We judge
with the impatience that comes from the three scanty twenty-
year cycles which make up the life of a man; man is impatient,
life does not worry, it has plenty of time.

Let's remember that after the year 1000 the reviving world
campaigned with an immense enthusiasm. And that, in order to
create the new naves of the churches, they looked back to the
Romans and made the Romanesque. And that one day the true
method, the pointed arch, appeared in the groin of a vault, and
that suddenly they understood and leaped forward. There was
liberation in that vault rib. The cathedrals were born.

Our world may be ugly, may be false, may be cruel. Nevertheless, everything is being tried out, everything is in movement,
is unfolding. The reason for things will appear—or has appeared
—in the hollow of its hand, and the light of hurrying days reveals constructive values. There may be labels of all kinds. Parti-
sans may demand timely or paralyzing orthodoxies. In the display
of the forces of the world, the machines that are useful appear.
If the USSR on the steppes, in its vast empty spaces, over its exceptional distances, has the time to meditate on pure ideas, the
USA, in the rush of colonization and in the busyness of this century of machines which was born at the right moment, has dem-

onstrated the limitlessness of our realizable hopes. The proofs are there. The world is ill as a result? A victorious boxer offers a most discouraging and pitiable spectacle: swollen face, disheveled hair. Tomorrow, washed and rested, he is *the champion!*

The machine is champion and the new times are here.

Let us square up good, well-made, healthy plans, in the service of men.

"I should like to bring to an examination of conscience and to repentance those who, with all the ferocity of their hatred, of their fright, of their poverty of spirit, of their lack of vitality, concern themselves with a fatal stubbornness in the destruction and hindrance of whatever is most beautiful in this country—France —and in this period: the invention, the courage, and the creative genius occupied especially with questions of building—with those things in which . . . wisdom and enterprise join hands."

"When the cathedrals were white [as they once were] Europe had organized the crafts under the imperative impulse of a . . . technique . . ."

Where can the young go? They are experiencing the mirage of exoticism. In their minds they are creating imaginary paradises. For them—here at home—everything is abominable; far away there is a land flowing with milk and honey where men are angels. . . . This is what I should like to say to the young:

Look within yourselves and recognize that you come from a milieu which is indissolubly associated with all your sensations and all your efforts. Do not repudiate it. Do not imagine that elsewhere there are no wolves and that love abounds. Exoticism? From many experiences I know how immediately enchanting it is. But there are the same reasons for enchantment in the essence of things which are your own milieu; for a moment, draw back far enough to survey your milieu as it is, in its reality. In it you will find the depths of the reason for things on which you are based and you will feel profound love and a great desire to bring them into the light of the beautiful today. It is here that you must do your work; a healthy, logical, inventive, joyous work, full of the essential virtues, in harmony with your line of life. Machine civilization has begun; it is a new age of humanity. The greatest proportions, the most vast dimensions can be achieved. It is a great adventure; it extends over the whole world, which is in a process of renewal. In the calendar of the world, each human group, differently situated in relation to the sun, through the division of peoples, through still imperceptible causes or tangled circumstances, will do its work. The telegraph has brought everything closer, but the seas are always barriers. Northerners react differently from Africans. The steppes have an effect on men which is different from that of hills, mountains, or seas. The fir tree and the palm lead to varied poetics.

"A new age has begun. A new Middle Age. Through the blood and the sufferings of battles, we must observe the flawless unfolding of the creative work. The interior, the fabric, the nave of the cathedrals was purity itself, but the outside was organized like an army in battle, as hirsute as an army.

"Technique has given us boldness and daring in rational tasks. Let's break the constraint on our hearts; let's drive away the agony of the unknown; let us draw up the human and poetic plans of the new world. Let's reconstruct everything: the roads, the ports, the cities, the institutions. The page has turned and enough material proofs have been furnished by the accomplishments of this century to assure us that we should see greatly and aim high.

"Above all, let us build for ourselves a new consciousness. That effort does not have a collective basis or character. It finds its support in the depths of each person, in the silence of individual self-examination; great sacrifices may be required in order that this new consciousness, aroused everywhere, may be the great universal consciousness, the lever of fruitful deeds."

Catalog

If you are interested in a list of fine Paperback
books, covering a wide range of subjects
and interests, send your name and address,
requesting your free catalog, to:

McGraw-Hill Paperbacks
330 West 42nd Street
New York, New York 10036